SURREY VOL I

Edited by Steve Twelvetree

First published in Great Britain in 2003 by
YOUNG WRITERS
Remus House,
Coltsfoot Drive,
Peterborough, PE2 9JX
Telephone (01733) 890066

SB ISBN 1 84460 259 1

FOREWORD

Young Writers was established in 1991 as a foundation for promoting the reading and writing of poetry amongst children and young adults. Today it continues this quest and proceeds to nurture and guide the writing talents of today's youth.

From this year's competition Young Writers is proud to present a showcase of the best poetic talent from across the UK. Each hand-picked poem has been carefully chosen from over 66,000 'Hullabaloo!' entries to be published in this, our eleventh primary school series.

This year in particular we have been wholeheartedly impressed with the quality of entries received. The thought, effort, imagination and hard work put into each poem impressed us all and once again the task of editing was a difficult but enjoyable experience.

We hope you are as pleased as we are with the final selection and that you and your family will continue to be entertained with *Hullabaloo! Surrey Vol I* for many years to come.

CONTENTS

A Winter Poem

Winter is the best season
Birds fly to the west
Leaving their nests.

When it snows children are so happy,
So am I.
Throwing snowballs everywhere.
The laughter of everyone,
and the enjoyment, you can tell
that winter has come.

The wind is ice cold.
Trees and bushes are waving
and swaying all about.
Trees looking so pretty.

Emma Hill (11)
Clewborough House School

Pepper - (My Cat)

In she comes through her little door,
A little cry then a roll on the floor
It's time for food, she lets me know,
Don't delay I want to go.
Fish she hates it's meat for her,
Then a fuss and a purr.

Her yellow eyes look so bright and proud,
Her cry is squeaky, but awfully loud.
A coat that's black and shines so well,
She looks so healthy we can tell.
She's the best cat we all agree,
Life without her would be misery.

Caroline Davies (11)
Clewborough House School

WINTER

Winter is the best,
You have to wear a vest.
It's too cold to go out,
You know what winter's about.

It often snows,
And the cold wind blows.
The snow goes *creek*
Under your feet.

Your feet go numb
While you go dumb.
Your nose goes red,
You want to be in bed.

All the animals are gone
Including the beautiful swan.
Most of the trees
Have no leaves.

Natalie Hilton (10)
Clewborough House School

WINTER WONDERLAND

Snowflakes, snowflakes falling to the ground
Everywhere is white and there is not a sound
Maybe the snow will stay
So Jess and I can play
We could throw snowballs
While the snow falls
Or we can make a snowman
I like that plan!

Rebecca Wycherley (9)
Clewborough House School

SNOWMANIA

Snowmania, Snowmania,
Welcome to Snowmania
Play in the snow
Get white as snow
It's all out in Snowmania!

It's time to play
To take up the day
In Snowmania . . .
In Snowmania . . .
All you do is play.

There are so few at school today
It's like an everlasting play
Huh, what's that?
I say what's that?
Oh no! We're trapped in school today!

Luke Simpson (8)
Clewborough House School

SNOWFALL

Have you seen outside today?
We couldn't go to school
Look outside! It's snowing!
It's broken a boring rule!

Go outside, go outside
Let's go outside and play
Go outside, go outside
Have you seen the snow today?

Stephanie Buzdygan (8)
Clewborough House School

Snowfall

Snowflakes falling,
Winding with the snow
Gather and gather to
Drop on the floor.

My friends and I go
Out to play throwing snowballs
On the way.

Snowflakes have stopped
Everybody's sad walking
Up and down the silent streets.

Ding-dong on the bell
Everybody's happy
The snow has started again.

It keeps on stopping, starting
Everything is in my mind
All this snow is giving me a heart attack.

Katie Hill (9)
Clewborough House School

War In Iraq

W orried faces in Iraq
A merica is ready for war
R ain adding to our gloom.

I mportant businesses have no one working
because they have gone to war
N uclear traces have been found in Iraq.

I nnocent people hurt
R ationing food and petrol would soon happen
A rmed forces arriving
Q uestioning people all around in Iraq.

Laurence Moss (11)
Clewborough House School

Waking Up To Snow . . .

When I woke up today,
Well, when I woke up today
It was a glistening grotto
Not a blizzard or an icy igloo.

There were bits of Heaven falling down
Lonely footprints and sledge land.
Trucks were stuck.
Shake me awake!
Just a dream . . . let's wait . . .

Holly Alsop (9)
Clewborough House School

Having Fun In The Snow!

Have you seen outside today?
Look at the weather,
Let's go play!
Let's stay up all night
Then again we could have a snowball fight!
Why don't we build a snowman?
I'll get the carrots,
You get the coal,
And you get some more people,
Because we'll build him really tall!
This is fun, let's carry on!
Don't get carried away
Be careful
Or we might have to stay
In all day!
Oh no, oh no,
We want to stay
Out all day
Oh well
Our day ends
We'll just have to wait
Till it snows again.

Cassandra Lazareff (9)
Clewborough House School

Dolphins

I was watching a dolphin show,
Tiny only jumped low,
A dolphin jumped and kissed a bow,
With a trainer in tow.

One poor dolphin didn't have a fin,
They named the dolphin Lynne.
The crowd clapped, what a din,
Poor finless Lynne tumbled right in.

The dolphin jumped extremely quick,
His tail gave a left flick,
It was an astonishing trick,
Performed so very slick.

Charlotte Hill (10)
Clewborough House School

Dogs Are Fun

Dogs are fun, dogs are cool.
Dogs like swimming in the pool.
Dogs are friendly, dogs are nice.
Dogs don't like eating mice.
Dogs are cute, dogs are soft.
Dogs like going in the loft.

Dogs are fun, dogs are cool.
Dogs like playing the fool.
Dogs are friendly, dogs are nice.
Dogs don't like freezing ice.
Dogs are cute, dogs are soft.
Dogs like hiding in the croft.

James Fuller (9)
Clewborough House School

JUNGLE DISASTER

My trip to the jungle was a disaster
the whole of my leg ended up in plaster
I acted like Tarzan and swung on a vine
I hadn't realised it was covered in slime.
I just happened to slide
then ended up on my side.

A gorilla grabbed me
and decided to flee
with me under his arms.
We swung through the palms.
My leg hit a tree
and the gorilla dropped me.
I screamed and yelped
But nothing seemed to have helped.

An hour later a kind orang-utan
came and took me away in a frying pan.
He was rather clever
and did not deter
to take me away to his nest.
This challenge put him to the test.

Now I'm in hospital
and it is not at all tropical,
this is the end of my disaster
where the whole of my leg ended up in plaster!

Molly Johnson-Jones (10)
Clewborough House School

PLACES

I went to Reading
to get my bedding.
I was pale
so I went to Wales.

I went to Surrey
to eat some curry,
Then I went to Norwich
to get more porridge.

I went to Bristol
to find some crystal
Then I went to Blackpool
to go in a swimming pool.

I went to Bath
to see their path
Then I went to Hull
to see a bull.

Mayuka Haga (10)
Clewborough House School

Up, Up Into The Sky

Up, up into the sky
I watch my kite
I watch it fly.

If the wind keeps blowing,
My kite will keep flowing.
But if the wind were to stop,
My kite will come down - *plop.*

I'd like it to stay there,
All day and all night.
I could tie it to a tree
To keep it in sight.

Up, up in the sky
To watch my kite
And watch it fly.

Matthew Smedley (9)
Clewborough House School

Touch!

(Touch)

Touch, what can you feel?
The wet feathers of a newborn chick.
The scaly skin of a snake.

(Touch)

Touch, what can you feel?
The wet skin of an earthworm.
The cold edge of a knife.

(Touch)

Touch, what can you feel?
The sharp edge of a broken glass.
The soft fur of a horse.

Zara Walker (9)
Clewborough House School

Listeners

(Based on 'The Listeners' by Walter De La Mare)

'Is there anybody there?' said the traveller,
Knocking on the rusty door,
And the footsteps of zombies
And the bloodstained floor.
'Is there anybody there?' he said
Knocking on the splintered door
And the crackling of a candle
And the buzz of a saw.

Joseph Cripps (9)
Grand Avenue Primary School

My Three Pets

I have a cat,
Who is ever so fat,
She scratches the mat,
And sleeps in a hat.
Her name is Pat.

I have a dog,
Who thinks he's a frog.
He went for a jog
He got lost in the fog,
Then we found him on a log.

I have a pig,
Who is ever so big,
And on his head, he wears a wig,
In his pen, he did a jig,
He turned round the corner, and started to dig.

Samuel Hopkins (9)
Grand Avenue Primary School

The Listeners

(Based on 'The Listeners' by Walter De La Mare)

'Is there anybody there?' asked the boy,
knocking on the moonlit door.
And the ghost peering over the sill.
As the knocker stared at him in the moonlight
and the ghost ready for the kill.

'Is there anybody there?' asked the boy.
And he opened the door.
As he went in the ghost was ready,
and he killed the boy with a dark saw.

Ben Akerman (10)
Grand Avenue Primary School

THE LOST BOY

'Are you there?' whispered the little boy,
Tapping on the dirty windows.
And a gust of howling wind
Lashing the huge trees branches.
And a brown mouse scuttled from under the door,
Squeaking and running around.
He tapped upon the window
And whispered once again.
Clouds of smoke billowed from the chimney,
Making the small boy cough.
He peeped in through the window
And what he saw was a fire blaze.
He tapped again, but this time on the door.
No one answered,
There was no noise,
There were no voices,
There was no sound.

Priya Ahluwalia (10)
Grand Avenue Primary School

THE LISTENERS

(Based on 'The Listeners' by Walter De La Mare)

'Is there anybody there?' says the traveller
Knocking on the moonlit door.
And the shadows creep past the traveller
And the thunder begins to roar.

'Is there anybody there?' says the traveller
Knocking on the moonlit door.
And the traveller begins to feel cold
And his head begins to feel sore.

Nicola Hudson (10)
Grand Avenue Primary School

The Listeners

'Can I have some milk?' cried the lonely lost child,
Knocking on the sunlit door.
And the sun blaring at the little child,
And the cats purring at the little child.
'Is there anybody there?' cried the lonely lost child,
Knocking on the moonlit door
And the door creaked open,
And there laid by the door was some milk and bread.

'Help me, help me' wailed the poor old woman,
Banging on the moonlit door.
And the wind pushing her off her feet,
And the owls hooting, scaring the poor old woman.
And she ran away,
And the phantom listeners hear her run.

Anisha Patel (9)
Grand Avenue Primary School

The Listeners

(Based on 'The Listeners' by Walter De La Mare)

'Is anybody there?' said the traveller,
Knocking on the moonlit door,
And the doorknocker staring at you.

The phantoms listening to the traveller,
And the skeleton awakening too.

Travellers pass by looking at this house,
Phantoms looking at the street,
And the street still looking at this house.

Sharmili Satkunam (9)
Grand Avenue Primary School

The Smugglers Song

Don't look at the bearded men,
They are running to their secret den
They take stuff from little girls,
And go around stealing precious pearls.

If you hear them shouting out loud,
You'll suddenly see a very big crowd.
They've got swords and muskets and deadly guns,
And then they go home and teach their sons.

And their daughters watch in vain,
as their fathers go galloping in the rain.
As they gallop and they ride,
They go in houses and they hide.

Alia Rehman (9)
Grand Avenue Primary School

The Traveller

'Is anybody there?' said the traveller
Knocking on the moonlit door,
And the wind ruffled his curly hair,
As the trees crashed to the floor.

'Is anybody there?' he said a second time,
Standing on the porch.
But no one came to answer him.
With candle light or torch.

Then suddenly he shouted out,
'I will not come again.'
And then he got up on his horse and galloped
Through the rain.

Emily Finch (9)
Grand Avenue Primary School

PHANTOM LISTENERS

(Based on 'The Listeners' by Walter De La Mare)

'Hello, hello is there anybody there?'
Called the woodcutter,
Knocking on the rusty old door.
And the howling wind
Blowing the leaves from the ferny floor.
And in the moonlight
Bloodstained curtains swishing from side to side.
And deep in the mansion,
Where the phantoms hide,
The woodcutter's brave feel is scattering,
While the phantoms
Hear the voice of the woodcutter chattering.
The woodcutter shouted, 'I came and I kept my word,'
Then the phantoms heard footsteps on the stony ground.

Oliver Cripps (9)
Grand Avenue Primary School

THE GROOVY FISH

I had a fish called Tango,
Which was my favourite fish,
But on my birthday poor Tango died,
Because the cat had him on his dish.

I write this poem for my fish,
I hope you like it best,
But if you find it in your heart,
To pay your best respects.

Nadine Thuraisingham (9)
Grand Avenue Primary School

My Parrot

My parrot is puffy and fluffy,
he's very tame
and never a pain.
You might get a bite
If you give him a fright.
He's really talky
and always squawky,
just like what a parrot should be.

He's blue and gold
not big or bold
he eats nuts
and likes Pizza Huts
just like what a parrot should be.

Rio Edwin (9)
Grand Avenue Primary School

Cats, Dogs, Birds And Insects

I am not cleaning the birds' feathers,
I am not cleaning the dogs' spits,
I am not cleaning the cats' dish,
I am not cleaning the slugs' slime,
especially the spiderwebs.

What annoying cats, dogs, birds, slugs and spiders
Get me out of this mess!

Anna Khan (8)
Grand Avenue Primary School

The Woodcutter's Trip

'Is anyone in?' shouted the woodcutter,
Knocking on the windowpane
And a flicker of light shone through the window,
And the floorboards from the inside creaking.
And the rustling of ivy catching his eye,
And his horse was munching, munching, munching
In the darkness.
And he knocked once more,
'Is anyone in?' shouted the woodcutter, more scared.
A puff of smoke came pushing out of the chimney
And the gate went *clatter, clatter* in the wind.
And the woodcutter knocked, a third time.
But no head looked over the window,
And nobody opened the door.
And the crumbling brickwork falling,
Because of the sound of the ghosts,
And the movement of the leaves,
Dancing in the darkness,
As the woodcutter was gone.

Carrera Johnson (10)
Grand Avenue Primary School

Mitten The Kitten

Mitten has some fluffy paws,
Tortoiseshell is the colour,
She'll jump like a professional jumper,
And she won't say no to a treat,
She hides behind the banister,
Then pounces on her prey,
Mitten can be nice but she likes
To anchor you to the chair.

Kieran Oliver (8)
Grand Avenue Primary School

THE DARK RIDER

(Based on 'The Listeners' by Walter De La Mare)

'Is there anybody there?' whispered the Dark Rider,
Tapping on the shattered window frame.
And his horse behind him listening in the gusty wind,
While chewing the swaying grass.
And a bat shot out of the turret,
Skimming the rider's hair.
And the rider sneaked up on the crumbling bricks
Of the cracked house.
'Is anybody there?' the rider repeated.
But no one approached the rider
And there was no face peering through the window
Upon the spiders and slugs.
But from beyond the crumbling walls,
A spooky laugh filled the silence of the house.
And the noise of a howling ghost spooked the night air.
So the rider sat upon his horse
And the clatter of iron on stone
Sounded the way of the rider,
As he trotted into the dark forest and vanished.

Thomas Hinkley (10)
Grand Avenue Primary School

KITTEN CARE

Kitten care,
Kitten care,
Kittens, kittens everywhere,
Kittens far,
Kittens near,
Kittens home,
Kittens here.

Alicia Elmer (9)
Grand Avenue Primary School

The Beggar In Distress

(Based on 'The Listeners' by Walter De La Mare)

'Let me in!' yelled the distressed beggar,
Pleading for money and food.

And a howling hunter dog
Came creeping through the gloomy forest.

And the beggar's dirty blanket
Was ripped and rotting to bits.

And a bulky badger
Shot into his burrow underground.

As he banged on the door once again,
The ghostly people peeped through the window.

The beggar sat down on the dusty ground,
Scratching at his head.

They looked through the window again,
Making ghostly sounds.

He walked away with whistling sounds behind him.

Sarah Robinson (10)
Grand Avenue Primary School

THE SPY

(Based on 'The Listeners' by Walter De La Mare)

'Anyone there?' called the spy,
Through the violent flurry of moonlit rain.
And there was a slight rustling in the forest,
As a furry fox fired through the ferny wood.
And ghostly voices echoed down the hallway
So the spy's accomplice ran away in fright.
He called again and banged on the rotting door,
'Anyone there?' he shouted at the top of his voice.
But there was no reply from the old, cracked house.
No sound, no voices, no noise.
But then through the pouring rain bellowed an eerie screech,
And a white mouse scuttled through a crack in the house,
And he could just see a mysterious glow through the mossy window.

Then he made out a host of ghosts,
He ran, leaving only a note behind him.

James Tyrrell (10)
Grand Avenue Primary School

THE RHINO

It's rough and tough,
with a very big horn.
And hunts its prey at the light of dawn.
It is big and fierce and grey all over,
And can run as fast as my Landrover!

It's heavy and strong,
And also very long.
So beware of the rhino.

James Proudlove (8)
Grand Avenue Primary School

The Rider

(Based on 'The Listeners' by Walter De La Mare)

'Is anybody there?'
The rider impatiently said
As he banged on the rusty door.
The deafening sound of the howling ghost,
Echoed through the hall,
Making him shiver.
In the dark moonlit night he heard the wind call,
His horse's black mane shimmered.
Smoke out of the chimney came tall,
Making him cough and splutter.
Bright flickers of light flashed around,
And made his eyes bleed,
As he galloped away with no answer at all.

Charis Lagopoulos (9)
Grand Avenue Primary School

The Farmer

(Based on 'The Listeners' by Walter De La Mare)

'Hello is anyone there?' said the farmer loudly,
Looking in the shining window.
And his dog barking sounded through the night air
On the forest's silvery path.
And the moon glowing brightly
Shining over the dark street,
And the blackbird's wings flutter
Over the farmer's head.
And the wind rustling through the tall green trees.
'Hello is anyone there?' said the farmer,
'I kept my word, I'll be back.'

Samantha Mason (10)
Grand Avenue Primary School

THE HORSEMAN'S RIDE

(Based on 'The Listeners' by Walter De La Mare)

'Is anybody there?' shouted the horseman,
Knocking on the old cracked window.
And his horse clacked his hooves together
And a puff of smoke pushing out of the chimney,
And the tatty old door swooshing to and fro.
The horseman felt his heart thumping over and over again
And ghastly echoes followed the horseman down the haunted hallway,
And cobwebs continuously hanging on the wall,
The sound of screaming from the top of the building.
And he repeated 'Is there anybody there?
Is anybody there?' shouted the horseman,
Knocking on the old cracked window.

Emily McIlwain (9)
Grand Avenue Primary School

AT THE BEACH

We go to the beach to play,
All on a summer's day.
We love to roll about,
To jump and scream and shout.
We make a little stream,
As we put on our suncream.
The sun is as hot as a bean,
And we fly in our machine.
The sand is very rough,
But to face it you have to be tough.
We love to go to the beach,
And we love to play in the *sea!*

Meghan Butcher (8)
Holy Trinity CE Primary School

Warfare Poem

A mmo attacking from above
B ombs are banging and backjiving at us
C olonels being cheeky to Churchill
D ive bombers ducking and diving
E nergetic engines engage for lift off
F amilies fighting for their lives
G ermans gaily jumping for joy
H itler hopes he wins the war
I nside his ignorant body he knows he won't
J ittering jaws journey on
K amikaze bombers carry on killing
L ancasters launch liberal bombs
M esserschmitt makes more monstrous moves
N obody knows when it will stop
O pposite sides are always attacking
P eople plead peace on Earth
Q ueries are passed from country to country
R ationing races round the world
S pies surrender important info
T errible time was the war
U nfortunate countries under attack
V ital info is passed
W inning replaces worrying faces
X cited people exaggerate defeat
Y ugoslavians journey on
Z ooming Spitfires zap German Zeppelins.

Sebastian Smith & Bertie Ferns (10)
Holy Trinity CE Primary School

FOOTBALL PLAYERS

A is for Anelka always amazing
B is for Beckham brilliant and bold
C is for Cudicini classy and cool
D is for Dudek the dangerous daredevil
E is for Edu excellent and exciting
F is for Fowler fantastic and fabulous
G is for Gerrard graceful and great
H is for Henry happy and handy
I is for Inzaghi intense and inspiring
J is for Junior jumpy and jetty
K is for Kanu keen and kicking
L is for Ljungburg little and laudable
M is for Murphy mini and magic
N is for Neville nimble and nippy
O is for Owen observant and open-minded
P is for Pelé the perfect player
Q is for Quinn quick and quiet
R is for Ronaldinho raw and ravenous
S is for Seaman sorrowful and spectacular
T is for Tugay tiny and tricky
U is for Upson unbiased and unique
V is for Vassel vital and veracious
W is for Wright wonderful and wholesome
X is for Xavier who X-rays the pitch
Y is for Yorke young and youthful
Z is for Zola zealous and zestful.

Joel Woollard (10)
Holy Trinity CE Primary School

FEELINGS

A ngry is always aggressive and atrocious
B oredom is broken and bruised
C old is closed and cramped
D oubting is dainty and delicate
E mpty is employed because of Elizabeth
F at is frumpy and frustrated
G utted is gallant and geographic because of gas masks
H urt is hairy on Hallowe'en
I solated can be ignorant when ice skating
J ump is known to jerk when seen with Jester
K een is a kebab and keeps to a kennel
L ary is loud and loopy
M oany can be miraculous when managing a mansion
N osy is necessary to its niece
O stracised is open minded with its orchestra
P etrified can be a politician in Poland
Q uiet is quick and sometimes quarrelsome
R estful can be rotten and even rough
S leepy is Scottish and enjoys school
T ired is a tarantula teaching taughtology
U ncomfortable is understood because of an umpire
V ulnerable is verb in view
W et is watery in whales
X cited is my xylophone
Y earning is a yo-yo
Z estful as a zombie in the zoo.

Lindsay Connell (11)
Holy Trinity CE Primary School

Football Players

A is for Anelka aiming into the goal
B is for Beckham big and bold
C is for Cheyrou cool and calm
D is for Diao dangerous and daredevil
E is for Edu excellent and egg-like
F is for Fowler frantic and fouling
G is for Gerrard great with goals
H is for Henry hasty and handy
I is for Inzaghi influential person
J is for Jeffery jumpy and jetty
K is for Kanu king of kicking balls
L is for Ljungberg little and light
M is for Murphy mix and magical
N is for Neville with a nobbly nose
O is for Owen opaque and operative
P is for Pires a perfect player
Q is for Quinn quiet and quick
R is for Riise remote and resentful
S is for Smicer small and sensitive
T is for Traore tall and tricky
U is for Upson unattractive person
V is for Veron who volleys it very fast
W is for Wright war like wave
X is for Xavier who plays the xylophone
Y is for Yorke young and youthful
Z is for Zola who zigzags around the pitch.

Daniel Hughes (11)
Holy Trinity CE Primary School

Countries

A ustralia is always active and atrocious
B razil is the best at basketball
C anada can cut the cream ribbon
D enmark is dented down the drain
E gypt is where eight Easter eggs exploded
F rance is frightful and furious
G ermany has germs which are gentle and graceful
H ungary is hygienic and hairy
I taly is imaginative and impatient
J apan is jumpy and joyful
K enya has kicking kangaroos and knitting koala-bears
L ithuania is lumpy and lame
M ongolia has mad monkeys and monstrous muscles
N igeria is naughty and nice
O ceans are like Olympics jumping over octopuses
P oland has popping polar bears panting while pouncing
Q uebec has a queen as quiet as a quilt
R omania has rushing romance with rhinos
S weden have stomping snakes
T asmania has turquoise twisting turnips
U nited Kingdom is unified and unanimous
V ienna is vile and vicious
W ales has water warming the whales
Y ugoslavia has yapping yo-yos.
Z imbabwe has zigzag zebras.

Emily Sanders (10)
Holy Trinity CE Primary School

Sunny's My Dog

I have a dog, his name is Sunny.
He makes us laugh 'cos he's so funny.
When we go for walks in the park,
We always get home after dark.

If you scratch his belly, he shakes his leg,
If he wants a biscuit, he can sit up and beg.
When the postman knocks he will bark and bark,
Then bites his leg, just for a lark . . .

He stops for a wee at every tree,
And chases every squirrel that he can see.
He likes to swim in the lakes,
And cover me in mud when he shakes.

He follows me wherever I go,
And I will always love him so.
He makes me happy when I'm sad,
Sunny's the best friend I ever had!

Annie King (8)
Holy Trinity CE Primary School

My Cute Kitty

My cute kitty she walks around at night
With her silky fur gleaming like moonlight.
Her claws as sharp as knives as she itches off her fleas
And in the morning
She gets her breakfast
And says please!

Amy Champion (8)
Holy Trinity CE Primary School

My Hamster

My thin little hamster
Runs on her exercise wheel
We give her lots of nuts to eat
They are her favourite meal.

She tickles my hand
With her tiny feet
We keep her house tidy
We keep it all neat.

Her coat is very soft
And very very fluffy
And when we bathe and dry her
Her fur goes nice and puffy.

Her sharp pointed teeth
Can cut through her food
But when she's upset
Beware of her mood.

She's the best little pet
That we ever had
But when she does wrong
We get very mad.

Rebecca Champion (8)
Holy Trinity CE Primary School

Hip Hip Hooray

When the sun shines a torch of ray
All the children shout,
'Hip hip hooray.'
The thunder's loud
The lightning's bright,
The children don't look
Until it is out of sight.
When it rains there is no play,
And they have to stay in all day.
When the snow falls on the trees
It looks lovely enough to sneeze.
But if I could have the sun every day
I would shout,
    'Hip hip hooray.'

Lee Fettin (8)
Holy Trinity CE Primary School

An Animal Poem

Cats, cats, cats,
Big cats, small cats, they come in all different sizes.
I hear them miaowing at night
They come in different colours
I love cats!

Cats, cats, cats
They're always licking themselves
They like to play with strings and balls
Purring day and night
They like to chase mice and eat them
Cats, cats, cats.

Rianna Alleyne (9)
Holy Trinity CE Primary School

TIGER TIGER

Tiger tiger in the golden grass,
Tiger, tiger I know you're there,
Tiger, tiger, though you're camouflaged,
Tiger, tiger, I see your glare.

Tiger, tiger, beautiful tiger,
Why are you so fierce?
Why not be nice and kind and cuddly,
So that I can scratch your ears.

Tiger, tiger, terrible tiger,
If you don't change your ways,
Tiger, tiger, you'll meet your doom,
In a matter of days.

Tiger, tiger, you've had your chance,
But I will not bring my gun,
On second thoughts it might be best for me
    to turn and run!

Heather Johnston (10)
Holy Trinity CE Primary School

CHRISTMAS REUGA

Jesus has been born
Everyone is happy now
We have a good time.

Merry Christmas, everyone
Hope you have a lot of fun.

Santa is coming
Children are wrapping presents,
Christmas trees are great.

Zoe Allen (9)
Holy Trinity CE Primary School

THE LEOPARD

The leopard walks stealthily across the forest floor,
Making no sound towards its prey.
Its claws swipe at a small angry buzzing fly,
It walks swiftly clearly not wanting to be seen,
The sun scorching her hunched back.
Now the leopard moves swiftly in search of its camouflaged prey
that has hidden.
The palm trees rustle in the light breeze,
Her sharp eyes are watching alert,
She runs and hides behind a spider bush,
She clambers up a hollow tree,
Her eyes sensing danger,
She spots,
Chasing at fifty miles per hour,
Pounce! She misses,
The leopard is the master of tricks,
No animal can outwit it,
Her prey is desperate not
wanting to be caught,
She is getting more hungry,
A giant leap she lands on it,
Now she tucks into her well deserved prey,
How she has been longing.
She had been starving,
In the African plain.

Sarah Skeels (10)
Holy Trinity CE Primary School

Memories

I sit beside the fire and think
Of people long ago
Of summers that I have never seen
And springs I will never know.

I sit beside the fire and listen
Of noises all around me.
Of leaves that are falling
From the big oak tree.

I sit beside the fire and look
Of times that pass by
Of the cold hard world
That no one has yet realised.

Laura Price (10)
Holy Trinity CE Primary School

In My Dreams

In my dreams there's a land of possibilities
In my dreams is a world of happiness and joy
In my dreams is a place full of laughter
In my dreams there's no hurt or sorrow
In my dreams around every corner is a smile
In my dreams there is endless fun.
In my dreams you live yourself a gentle life
In my dreams is a place of hope
In my dreams is a world with bright sunshine
In my dreams is a land of peace
In my dreams is where I want to be every day.

Joanna Michael (10)
Holy Trinity CE Primary School

A Game Of Life

Boys, girls and parents
Dressed in white tennis clothes
Carrying big bags, heavy bags.

Tennis, tennis, tennis
What a sport
Scared, concentrate, focus
Tension all over the players.

Come on, come on, play well
What a challenge,
Have to win, need to win,
Need to prove myself, need to be the best.

Concentrate, keep thinking and focus
Serve and play with all your heart
Forehand, backhand, volley,
Move forward and kill the ball.

Tired, exhausted and sweating
Think and take your time
At last the end, the match has finished,
What a struggle, what a win.

Muhammad Bhimji (10)
Holy Trinity CE Primary School

Sweets

Some are sticky and some are hard
And some even have a collector's card.
Everlasting gobstoppers and brightly coloured chews.
Out of all of them it's toffee that I choose.

Matthew Love (9)
Holy Trinity CE Primary School

BATHROOM DISASTER

Oh what a laugh,
When Mum had a bath,
She called to her daughter,
'Sophia where's the water?'
I turned on the spout,
But nothing came out.
And as I had feared,
It had all disappeared.
So, I had an idea . . .
I got Dad's beer
And filled the tub,
For Mum to scrub,
And oh my golly,
Was my mum jolly.

Sophia Horgan (8)
Holy Trinity CE Primary School

THE TIGER

The big giant paws the size of my head
The rock hard ground as her bed
Her long long teeth lovely and white
Soft silky coat, oh what a sight.
Hunted by man
Shotgun in hand
As her friend
I say
This is the end.

Bethany Dunn (9)
Holy Trinity CE Primary School

Sheltie

His coat is golden as the autumn leaves and
as smooth as the sand washed by a blanket of sea.
He gallops like a steam train when he comes
rushing over to greet me.

Carrots, peppermints and apples are his favourite food.
He's as gentle as a butterfly when he eats out of my hand.
He's a pony with a big heart.
We enjoy adventures together across the land.

His name is Sheltie and Shetland is his breed.
He's as cute as a puppy.
Sheltie is my pony and he is everything I need.

Hannah Butters (8)
Holy Trinity CE Primary School

Best Friends

B est friends is where the friendship never ends
E asy breaking up with a friend, but not with a best friend
S pecial to each other
T rusting each other all the time.

F alling out breaks your heart
R ecalling old memories
I ncreasing your friendship every day
E njoying each other's company
N ever letting down a best friend
D on't keep secrets from each other
S o now you know, how to become a true
Best Friend.

Sanna Khan (10)
Holy Trinity CE Primary School

STRETCH

Stretch your toes,
Stretch your legs,
Dance to the music.

Smile till your
Cheekbones hurt,
Dance to the music.

Stretch, Stretch, Stretch
Don't lean back and
Don't stick your ribs out.
Don't want to see what
You had for dinner
Or that
Big fat bum
Of yours.

Amber Staniforth (8)
Holy Trinity CE Primary School

MY IMAGINARY HORSE

I have an imaginary horse
I imagine him on the moors
Enjoying his grazing
He looks so amazing
How I love my imaginary horse.

I see my imaginary horse
Trotting amongst the gorse
In the sun having fun.
I wish he was really my horse.

Holly Tricklebank (8)
Holy Trinity CE Primary School

When I Grow Up

When I grow up I want to be
As strong as a fireman
As small as a flea.

I want to be a pirate
that sails all the seas
I want a friend called Lisa
But I'll call her Leas.

I want to be a pop star
like the Bee Gees.
I want to meet
other celebrities.

I want to look after animals
but I don't like bees
I want to play the trumpet
but not pay the fees.

When I grow up
I don't know what to be
I guess we'll just
have to wait and see.

Pinar Temiz (9) & Francesca Morgan (10)
Holy Trinity CE Primary School

UNDER THE SEA

A ngelfish anchoring acorns
B ig boats banging badly
C atfish catching cod
D olphins diving dangerously
E lectric eels eating elephants
F ishes frying French fries
G uppys gobbling goats
H ippos having hiccups
I ce inking igloos
J umping jellyfish juggling
K ite kicking kittens
L eeches licking lemons
M ermaids making magic
N aked newts knitting
O range octopuses ordering oranges
P ink pikes picking pearls
Q ueen Quark
R ainbowfish rocking rods
S ea horses snoring silently
T wo turtles talking
U gly unhappy flea
V essels violently invading
W hales water walls.

Chloe Reeves (9) & Candice Wakerell (10)
Holy Trinity CE Primary School

UNDER THE SEA

Under the sea there are -

A n awful aqua angelfish asleep,
B army brills bashing boxes,
C ool catfish catching cod,
D otty dopey dangling dolphins,
E leven eels eating eggs,
F our friendly fish flirting
G ormless goldfish guiding guests
H undreds of hectic herrings hoping
I rresistible icebergs itching indignantly
J umping jellyfish juggling jugs
K ind kites kicking knitting
L imbering lings lurking low,
M ad mermaids mussing mussels,
N asty necklaces nibbling nuggets
O range octopuses obsessed with oranges
P erfect pikes picking pearls
Q uirky quarks quarrelling over quizzes
R ed rainbow-trouts rolling round
S even silly salmon singing
T en tacky tuna tickling
U pset urchins uniting umbrellas
V exed vessels viewing videos
W hite whitebait whirling and whooping
X citable X-ray fish xylophoning exceptionally
Y ellow yachts yelling at yaks
Z esty zebra-danios zooming in zigzags . . .
And probably hundreds of others!

Alice Ahearn (9) & Sarah Mathialahan (10)
Holy Trinity CE Primary School

Tears Of Terror In World War Two

Last night was a terrible night
The sirens,
Then the silence,
Then the shaking.
My eyes flashed before me
As nightmares emerged.
The flames,
The fire,
The upset screams.
They terrified me.
The tears became puddles
The air became smoke,
The ground became dust,
As I found myself wondering
Would I be here tomorrow?

Alexandra Elson (10)
Holy Trinity CE Primary School

A Messy Family

Mums, dads, sisters, brothers,
Aunties, uncles, fathers, mothers.
Cousins, babies, boys and girls
Freckled faces, ginger curls.
Rabbits, bunnies hop hop hop
Hunters chop chop chop.
Chocolate and sweets all around
Not a clean thing to be found
Socks and vests everywhere
All there is is underwear.

Temi Akinmade (9)
Holy Trinity CE Primary School

SCHOOL KID

I'm a school kid
that's never forbid
but has nits
in little bits.
Though I do have money
that shines like honey.
I have a sister
that looks like Mister (***)
I have a cousin
but another dozen
and have a brother
but when do I bother?
I watch Brum
I have a mum
that looks so dumb
but reads books
about her stylish looks.
I have a dad
that lost his pad
and went so mad.
I looked around
and saw on the ground
My dad's pad.
He said, 'Good lad.'
I have a friend
that made a mend
to my toy
just like a boy
and have a neighbour
that looks sour.

Jishnu Suriyakmaran (8)
Holy Trinity CE Primary School

WAR

The fear I could taste,
The lump in my throat,
And the taste of salty tears.
The soil and mud dried out my mouth.
The metallic taste of my shelter poisoned me
As my nightmares came alive.

The smell of fumes
And smoke around killed the air.
My nose was blocked
The smell of my mum's perfume
On my blanket.
All these smells were trapped in our shelter.

The screaming and crying
Was all too loud.
My small ears were filling with noises.
The crackles of fire and bombs exploding,
Sirens were whining
And the silence blackened the night sky.

The feel of my mum's cold hands,
Froze my body.
The soggy wet mud between my fingers and toes.
The dampness,
The coldness,
And the worst of all the sharp pain in my heart.

The sight I saw,
Made me cry in pain.
The fire,
Dead bodies,
The tears rolling down cheeks hopelessly
As my life flashed before me.

Laura-Jayne Clifford (10)
Holy Trinity CE Primary School

MUMMY AND DADDY

They help me with my homework
They do it very well
Maths, English, topic and teach me how to spell.

Mummy runs Brownies, every Tuesday night
Daddy goes bell ringing and meetings every night.

I help them get the plates out.
I help them cook the food.
It's best when it's macaroni cheese,
My favourite food.

They read me stories at bedtime,
They love me very much.
Stories, toys and cuddles and they
Kiss me goodnight.

Ruth Gunnell (8)
Holy Trinity CE Primary School

THE DRAGON

As the dragon furiously flies in the night's darkness.
The dragon awaits its prey,
The rain falls like bullets from the sky.
Lightning strikes rapidly,
pure white snow overflowing the village.
In the pitch-black night the dragon awaits
But nothing moves in return.
As night turns to day and day turns to night
He has hunger but no feast has he.
The dragon takes his last breath and falls!

Ryeed Rahim (9)
Holy Trinity CE Primary School

War Never Ends

What a big mistake I made
Coming home to the war
Even though the countryside
Was always such a bore.

People dying all around
Bombs being dropped,
All I can think about
Is when it will be stopped.

My father has gone away
Never to be seen again,
My mother is beside me
But her great despair is main.

The war has lasted six long years
My mistake has come to an end
Dropping down, hitting the floor,
My wound will never mend.

Becky Maguire (11)
Holy Trinity CE Primary School

Curry!

Everyone likes curry!
but do not worry
it has a spice
but very nice
so take a bite
and you will fall straight
asleep at night.
So no worry
it's only curry!

Emily-Louise Williams (9)
Holy Trinity CE Primary School

TWINS

Waa waa it's what they're best at
Waa waa I think you've guessed it,
Double the trouble day and night
Do you think it's a baby; well you got that right.
Is there a time where they don't make a din?
Crying and moaning equals twins.

Poo-poo, it's what they do
Wee wee, it's their cup of tea
It's not exactly worth a fight
If Mum doesn't do it, I might.
Once it's done it goes in the bin
Pooing and weeing equals twins.

Yum, yum food is their best chum
Yum, yum I guess they won,
'Just be patient,' Mum tries to say
When they do it it'll be the day,
It goes so quickly tin after tin
Eating and drinking equals twins.

Smile, smile it's worth it for a while
Goo, goo it's not that much but it makes the adults ooh and aah
They say Dad Da, Mum says 'No, Mum, Mum, Mum, Ma, Ma.'
Then they argue boys go *wa wa wa*
It lasts for a while they just wanna win
Smiling and cooing equals twins.

Twins, twins I've said it all
Twins, twins they're on the ball
Take it easy, it's not at its worst
When they're older you'll just wanna burst,
Truthfully they're not bad,
Even if they do *drive me mad!*

Samantha Lindars (10)
Holy Trinity CE Primary School

The Storm

Flash! Forked lightning rips through the sky
The clouds are angry dragons with flaming breath
Crash! There is their fire, tearing the sky in two
The lightning lashes the ocean.

Tormented, frantic waves
Whipped to a frenzy by the screeching wind
They are free and angry
Wild white stallions of foam and spray.

The boat is a sleek little mare fighting the ocean
She bucks, pitches and rears back up again
She plunges about in the maddened waters
Bravely battling the great sea.

The sky gradually clears to reveal
Brilliant beautiful blue
The warm sun smiles down on me
The storm has passed.

Zoë Hackett (11)
Longacre School

The Secret Place

My secret place is hidden in a cave,
Near a crystal clear stream.
And in that cave, five slender hollows,
Fit for a fairy king and queen.

The rich smell of moss that lies on the ground
And the tapestry of ivy on the wall,
This secret place that I have found
Where nobody goes at all.

Alice Antcliff (10)
Rydes Hill Preparatory School

FROST

The sun touched the horizon on a world of glimmering white
A sparkling kind of light,
Was lying on the ground.

Even though the sun was rising,
It was very agonising,
That the frost was as cold as could be.

Little pictures on the windowpane
Of a little lane,
Where fairy-tales live.

Who makes these little pictures of a little lane?
On the silver windowpanes?
Jack Frost of course. Who else?

He comes creeping with his tools,
He tries the door. He thinks Fools!
You cannot keep me out with locks and bolts,
For I am Jack Frost.

Under the door he squeezes
He never freezes
On a cold winter's night.

When he leaves
He does not grieve
For he will see you again.

Lucy Porter (11)
Rydes Hill Preparatory School

Growing Up!

He was just a little lion cub
His name was Bingalloo
He played all day
With his friend Cabay,
Under the sky so blue.

Everyday,
They played their games,
But one day they did not.

Today Cabay is all alone,
For Bingalloo has grown!

'No time to play today,' said Mum,
'Because you have to hunt!
Your father used to feed us all,
But now you bear the brunt!'

Hope Allen (10)
Rydes Hill Preparatory School

The Whirling Wind

It howls past the countryside
Destroying everything in its path.
Seeking prey and then pouncing,
Tearing it apart.
Then creeping under the moonlight
And speeding through the fields.
It pauses and gazes at the moon,
Letting out a long deep howl.
Turns back, retreats
And returns to its den.

Lucy Hart (9)
Rydes Hill Preparatory School

FROST

They creep around when we're asleep
Tucked up in our beds,
They nip our feet and climb our bodies,
Right up to our face,
And leap about freezing things
All through the night.

These tiny little people,
Jump around all night
'Til early in the morning
When everything is white.

When we wake in the morning,
Everything is white
Until later that day
When the sun comes out.

Jane Salmon (10)
Rydes Hill Preparatory School

THE SNOW

It falls like velvet feathers,
Into its empty nest.
As it swoops down without a sound,
And walks peacefully, as God's messenger.
It perches in every tree,
Bush,
Plant.
Not a single slash of dirt is seen.
Soon the sun shines down and reflects
The peaceful snow.

Rebecca Beasley (9)
Rydes Hill Preparatory School

A Cold Winter Snow!

In the morning I awoke to a winter's day,
To see some snow, while in bed I lay.
The trees were white with a sprinkle of green,
They were very beautiful and so was the scene.

I raced outside to the cold winter's snow,
As I wondered what had happened to the grass below.
I made a snowman with a carrot for his nose,
Buttons for eyes and sticks for his toes.

Everyone was now in the cold outside,
We bought a toboggan and went for a ride.
That had to be the highlight of the day,
As I thought that night while in bed I lay.

Emily Shortal (10)
Rydes Hill Preparatory School

Winter Poem

In wintertime all children go
Playing in the fields of snow,
Although it is cold they still have fun,
And all through the day,
They go and play
Out in the cold winter sun.

The children retire
To sit by the fire
When the sun is in need of a rest
Until the next day
It won't go away
It'll stay as a welcome guest.

Elizabeth Elsom (11)
Rydes Hill Preparatory School

When Everyone Is Asleep

When everyone is asleep,
Not making a peep,
Jack Frost comes out
And dances about.
Wherever he goes,
On his icy cold toes,
He turns everything white
All through the night.

Every puddle he will see,
Will drop a degree,
All the droplets he knows,
Will become his foes.
They will turn to ice,
In a trice.
They will glisten in the sun
Like nothing has been done.

When you awake,
From your break,
Your fingers and toes
Will have froze,
Because Jack Frost,
Has not lost,
His icy touch . . .
Much!

Lauren Holley (10)
Rydes Hill Preparatory School

Crystal Ice

Cobwebs hung with shining water beads,
Grasses sprinkled with sparkling dew
Houses draped with crystal ice
Winter frost is here.

Robins singing sweetly,
On the snow fallen tree
Tiny little snowdrops
Resting on their beaks.

Snowflakes gently floating
Slowly through the air,
Landing on the fields so white,
Covering them with care.

Deer prancing in the snow,
Having lots of fun
Keeping warm with their soft fur
Winter at last has come!

Isabelle Edmondson (10)
Rydes Hill Preparatory School

Drought

Sliding across the parched desert
Passing dried rivers and shrubs.
The sun beams on its long scaled body
Spreading over the sizzling ground
Drying everything.
Its tail flickers like the sunrays
Slowly and steadily it leaves.

Katie Silvester (10)
Rydes Hill Preparatory School

Jack Frost

Creeping around the corners,
Rattling at the windows,
Someone is out,
But who?

Is it next-door's cat,
Or is it the fox
Who is out?
Softly a voice answers.

'It is me Jack Frost,
Out on this night,
Come, hold my hand,
We will go for a glide.'

We fly through the sky,
Turn fields white,
Hang icicles from roofs,
And off trees.

It is like paradise,
As free as a bird,
Drifting through the sky,
Lit by the moon.

Frost lies sparkling,
A blanket of white,
What a wonderful ride,
This beautiful night.

Rebecca Dodds (11)
Rydes Hill Preparatory School

CHRISTMAS POEM

At Christmas time it's every child's dream
To see a winter wonderland scene
In front of their windows each and every day,
So that they can go out to play in the snow
All white and crisp with sparkles of blue.
One day this dream came true
And all the children came out to play
With snowballs in their hands
Or snowmen in their thoughts.
I went to have a walk
To think of the Christmas gone past
And to take in all the children's wonderful smiles.
As I walked I came across a little child.
I asked her why she was not playing in the snow.
She answered with a little mumble
'I have no family.'
I held out my hand and she took it.
From that day on I loved and cared for her,
As if she were my own.
And this is the meaning of Christmas,
Goodwill, joy and hope,
This is what I did for my homeless child.
And this is what Mary and Joseph did for their Holy child.

Eleanor Corcoran (10)
Rydes Hill Preparatory School

JACK FROST

Jack Frost of course is coming
He's coming on a cloud
He's shaking silver powder
And dancing all around.
He's running through the flower beds
And climbing all the trees
He's squeezing through the keyholes
And sliding under doors.

While we all are sleeping
Sleeping in our beds
Jack Frost is broadly smiling
And breathing on the windows.
As he breathes upon the windows
With his icy breath
He draws upon it snowflakes
Pretty, white and sparkly.

Then we people are awaking
Jack Frost's smile fades
He climbs back on his cloud
And hurries off away.
As I climb into my wellies
And put upon my scarf
I see Jack Frost smiling
Glinting in the sun.

Phoebe Young (10)
Rydes Hill Preparatory School

PRAYER BEFORE BIRTH

(Based on 'Prayer Before Birth' by Louis MacNeice)

I am not yet born; protect me.
From the devilish black death that falls upon me.
From the eight legged freak's black web of doom.
And save me from the skeleton's mount.

I am not yet born; O save me,
From the deadly desert.
The lion of unhappiness that makes me cry,
And the nightmare maker.

I am not yet born; provide me
With the rushing fresh water and the fruits,
Of the forest.
And a place that we can sleep in peace and not worry,
O guide me.

Alexandra Lewis (9)
Rydes Hill Preparatory School

A WORLD WITHOUT ANY SWEETS

Imagine there's a land without any sweets.
It would be terrible, never any sweets.
No sweets for pudding, no sweets for birthdays.

It would be disgraceful to have no sweets.
I would hate to live in a land without any sweets.
I would be crying every day.

I wouldn't like it at all.
Now, you would not like it to live in a land without
any sweets
And neither would I.

Tiffany Somerset-Wood (8)
Rydes Hill Preparatory School

At Night

Six o'clock
The early dusk rising
Up from the gazing green hills
The moon appeared,
Sitting in the silent still alleyways,
Where I was sleeping with the old
Rusty bins
Where the rat
And the cat
Scratching in the bins.
In the distance
The moon
Looking down, following me
Down the alleyway.

Lindsey Hackett (9)
Rydes Hill Preparatory School

A Land Without Sight

Imagine a land without any sight
We would be walking around in the dark not the light
We would be tripping all over things in the room
Sooner or later we would trip over a broom.

We would get blind by the dark
And imagine we were being chased by a shark
Do you know what I found under the stair
I found my old gandpa's chair.

We would pray and pray and beg and beg
Still nothing would move except a peg
So left with no light or warmth from the sun
Oh! What a world without any fun.

Amelia Hamilton (8)
Rydes Hill Preparatory School

Nature

Imagine a world with no nature
No pretty walk in the countryside
Down the cow's field but no grass at all
Then when it came very dark
There seemed to be a little spark
Then the air was very still.
And suddenly there seemed to be rain
Slowly, slowly the seeds we could see were very plain
And very slowly water started to flow higher and higher
There was too much water, the grass would not grow
The seeds were not high up like the water they were low
You would get so bored you would walk home
Nothing good to see, no flowers, no trees
And the wasp would be angry and so will the bees
Then what suddenly seemed to be
Nature, nature everywhere
Beautiful all around
Best as ever grass on the ground
You can be happy all the time
Hopping, skipping, everywhere
We love and care
And best of all we love our family
It's the best day in every way
And that's the best thing you could ever say
I do not know how to explain how wonderful today is.

Tiffany Dodds (9)
Rydes Hill Preparatory School

A World Without Homework

Dear Chief of Children's Education.

A world without homework
Is just not good enough
And I am certainly not chuffed
I will lose my job at work.

I would like my child to be intelligent
Instead of struggling trying to be top
A World Without Homework has to stop
At the moment my child is not a very good student!

All children will not be able to do their tables
Not even the alphabet
I bet!
At Christmas children won't know about Jesus and the stable.

No educated teachers to tell children off!
Just because homework does not exist
Yes that was a good career you just missed!
At Christmas homework does not exist so children could go out in the snow and catch a horrible cold!

At Easter they will not know about teeth
And will be eating millions of chocolate eggs
Do you want me to get down on my knees and beg?
You are no chief educator!

Now all children are not bright
Homework is good
And I think you should
Give up and say I am right!

A world without homework,
I am not very happy, not at all!
Half of my child's life was playing ball!
Anyway I have got to get on with my work.

Yours sincerely,

Sabrina Ouki (8)
Rydes Hill Preparatory School

THE SUN

It hovers in the sky
Yellow
Bright
Bringing joy to the world
Pleasure and hope.
It's cheerful as it looks down
Singing
Fluttering feathers descend gently
Like the sun's rays shining
It stops and looks a while
Then, slowly, it flies quietly back home
Sinking softly, it turns bright red.
It will get some sleep
Before tomorrow when it will rise again.

Charlotte Connor (9)
Rydes Hill Preparatory School

The Snow Fight

As I lay in bed
On a winter's day
I heard children laughing
While out at play.

As I opened my curtains
All I could see
Was a winter wonderland
So I screamed, 'Yippee!'

As I ran down the stairs
And out into the snow
I saw a snowball coming at me
So I ducked down low.

I picked up a snowball
Joining in the fun
Aiming at my friends
Who began to run!

Nicola Price (10)
Rydes Hill Preparatory School

At Night

Ten o'clock
We are still searching.
No single shed of hope.
We hunt in the forest,
For a particle of cloth.
Only a torch to light the way.
Awaiting for an alive child to carry, and
Some happy smiles to see.
A million tears gathered in my pocket,
And a soaking handkerchief.
Horrifying thoughts surround me,
And I can't bear to think.
Rustle!
Only a leaf brushing in the wind.
The night is dying
But no one is smiling.

Grace Osborne (9)
Rydes Hill Preparatory School

AT NIGHT

Two o'clock at night
I walk down the streets,
Looking for poachers with my long stick.
I see bright, shining, flickering lights
everywhere.
I'm carrying a faint lantern,
Things move around.
Footsteps walking closer to me.
Four o'clock,
Everything has faded away.
All the people have left
All the noises have faded down,
And the moon has gone.

Lisa Keelan (9)
Rydes Hill Preparatory School

AT NIGHT

Twelve o'clock, midnight
In a dirty, devilish dugout
A soldier in despair,
A single candle gives a milky glow to the dark, smoky night.
I try to concentrate on the one-hundredth letter to my wife
But the torturing, agonising cries of my comrades become too much.
I jump, but turn back to the letter, my hand shaking.
A whizzing noise, a flash of quick, bright light
Disturbs me once and for all.
A bomb has shattered the peace
No silence returns to no-man's-land
Five o'clock.
Daybreak ends the evil night
Bringing light but no happiness.
As fighting commences,
A bullet dodges, swerves and kills.
No one is winning,
The great world war.

Cerys Jenkins (10)
Rydes Hill Preparatory School

THE LAND OF MIDNIGHT GRAVITY

The land of midnight gravity
Where you float above the moon.
You will never get to stand
Where the funny mask goes on your face.
What if you wanted to do up your lace?
When you have the mask tight it hurts
and it tickles your face.
You're here to go at the gravity pace.
Where the moon is white and the sky is dark.
Where the little stars sparkle here and there
You wouldn't look for a much quieter place.

Now I'm in space floating high
I'm in a spacecraft
Floating at gravity pace it's so peaceful
and so graceful.

Victoria Rodwell (8)
Rydes Hill Preparatory School

Imagine A Land Without Any Sight

Imagine there's a land without any sight
You would have to feel your way up to your bed at night.
You wouldn't be able to run or play
You would have to stay in your room, in your bed all day.

When you wanted your breakfast,
You would go downstairs and trip and fall
And you would hardly be able to walk at all!

You wouldn't be able to go to the shops, to get your food,
And then you would probably go into a horrible mood.
Then when you wanted to go home, you would have to get a taxi
And then you wouldn't find your pockets to pay him your money!

It would *not* be nice to not be able to see with your eyes,
I find it is *much* better to
Have your sight.

Natalie Allee (8)
Rydes Hill Preparatory School

THE EMPTY WORLD

Imagine
A world
Where there is no sight.

Wouldn't it be terrible?
Especially at night
In this world
You see no light.

Not through the day and
Not through the night
You might bump
Into things and get a terrible fright!

All that is heard
Is the whistling of the air
Never ever a word
Has been heard.

Alice Gribble (8)
Rydes Hill Preparatory School

IMAGINE!

Imagine a land without any television!

I could be sick and jump up and down,
If I could I would run down town.
People would shout but not with glee,
If I could say 'It's not to do with me!'
I don't like the sound of it,
Having no television.
I don't like it one little bit, so fix it and quick!

Imagine a land without any toys!

I could be sick and jump up and down,
If I could I would run down town,
Children would pout and not know what to do,
They would simply mope and not know how to cope,
I don't like the sound of it,
Having no toys
I don't like it one little bit, so fix it and quick!

Imagine a land without any sweets!

I could be sick and jump up and down,
If I could I would run down town,
Only broccoli and carrots and healthy foods to eat,
No chewing gum, chocolate bars or any such treats,
I don't like the sound of it
Having no sweets
I don't like it one little bit so fix it and quick!

Carys Newbury (8)
Rydes Hill Preparatory School

A Land Without Sweets

Just imagine a land without
Sweets!

There would be fruit, vegetables
And savoury food.

No one would be able to have a party with proper party food.

Not even sweet prizes, party bags or pudding! It would be awful.

Just imagine a land without sweets!

All the mums and dads would say, 'Go and have some crackers,'
or, 'Go and have some fruit!'
Instead of saying, 'Go and have one biscuit!' or, 'Go and have a piece of shortbread!'

Just imagine a land without sweets!

It would be so awful! We wouldn't have enough energy.
Really it would be awful!

No one would want to live there, so it would be such a lonely place.
I would never go there!

Imagine a land without sweets!

Maisie Nowroz (8)
Rydes Hill Preparatory School

If I Were In A Place With No Sight

If I were in a place with no sight,
I'd be in darkness everyday.
I wouldn't see a bit of light,
My arms wouldn't be able to find their way.
Sometimes I'd go to the wrong house,
My parents would be worried sick.
I wouldn't be able to see a mouse,
They might think I was playing a trick.

If I were in a place with no sight,
I'd listen hard for birds and bees.
I wouldn't see a bit of light,
I might be able to hear the trees.
I'd be alone with not much to do,
A guide dog would be great company.
He'd help me when I am feeling blue,
And sit at my feet as I drink my tea.

If I were in a place with no sight,
I wouldn't think I'd like it at all.
I wouldn't see a bit of light,
So I think I'm better off in Bristol.
That way I know where I'm going,
And see the beautiful scenery.
Maybe I'll learn to do sewing
And have a bath and a cup of tea.

Christina Moh (9)
Rydes Hill Preparatory School

IMAGINE A LAND WITHOUT ANY TOYS!

Imagine a land
Without a toy shop
Children playing
With a mop.

No toys for girls
Or for boys
Not even a sign
Of any wind up toys.

No bears
No robots
Not even
Toy cots.

No game boards
No playing cards
No dolls houses
No toy farmyards.

No playdough
No clay
To have fun with
Today.

Fiona Armstrong (9)
Rydes Hill Preparatory School

A World Without Love

Imagine a world without any love,
Where no one acts like feelings exist.
All the people push and shove,
And people clench their fists.

People always fighting,
And going to war.
No families reuniting,
Nothing to even live for.

Everyone loses faith in each other,
And hearts always break.
No loving fathers or mothers,
So children on the streets fearfully shake.

People raise their guns,
And begin to shoot.
Soon the deed is done,
They have been such vicious brutes.

No one knows how to behave,
And people get carried away.
They use others like slaves,
So they die day-by-day.

We begin to wonder when the war will end,
And when life will be normal again.
When the hurt people's bones will start to mend,
And they will stop feeling the pain.

Finally things settle down
And what a relief that is.
But the city and town,
Have been destroyed because,

They did not love each other!

Caroline Elsom (9)
Rydes Hill Preparatory School

A World Without Schools

Imagine a world without any schools!
Every single one of us would just be big fools!
We wouldn't know how to count,
We wouldn't know how to spell.

I heard in the old days in France,
Life was just a trance,
Before they invented schools,
Yes, before they invented schools.

There would be no such thing as teachers,
There would be only slimy old leeches!
We would roam around freely,
Without anyone saying come and do your homework.

Though we need to go to school,
Life would be so cool . . .
With a world without any schools
Yes, a world without any schools!

Lilly Garrett (9)
Rydes Hill Preparatory School

A Land With No Gravity

Imagine if there was a land
With no gravity
Flying and floating about, how lovely
The sight is so beautiful
It is such a lovely feeling
Floating and flying about.

Imagine if there was a land
With no gravity
We would be floating and flying about
Within seconds
It would be wonderful
Floating and flying about.

Just imagine that!
Wouldn't it be lovely
Floating and flying about
The buildings and nature would look fantastic
We would have such a good view
Just floating and flying about.

Emma Hopkins (8)
Rydes Hill Preparatory School

THE LAND OF BLACK

Imagine there's a land where there isn't any sight,
It's just all black all day and all night.
So with your stick you move around,
And try not to fall over something on the ground.
Hear your stick go *tap, tap, tap,*
On something that is hard and then you find a small gap.
Squeeze through that and you'll make a noise,
To startle any more girls and boys.
Turn to your left or turn to your right,
But you can't see any light.
Oh no you think you're stuck,
Yuck, you've stepped in some muck.
Then you hear something,
It's a spring.
Find it and then have a drink,
And then you think.
That this is the end of the world,
This imaginary story is now told.

Lia Bucks (9)
Rydes Hill Preparatory School

Jack Frost

He dances and prances through the leaves,
He dances and prances where nobody sees.
He has sparkling fingers and sparkling toes,
He paints on the windows when nobody knows.

'Who is he?' I hear you ask,
He is the one who wears a mask.
For he is Jack Frost, who never gets lost,
He is the one who leaves us frost.

He breathes and the world shivers,
People wake up and find frozen rivers.
He dances and prances the night away,
But runs at dawn, runs from day.

As he dances and prances he leaves a trail,
Not at all like the one of a snail.
For his is cold and soft to touch,
This is snow, that everybody loves so much.

Soon his trail will melt away,
For the sun is not happy for it to stay.
Soon it will start to rain again,
And Jack Frost will hide in his den.

Helen Pearson (10)
Rydes Hill Preparatory School

Waterfalls

It starts easy
Gently going along
Then all of a sudden falls
Like a great lightning bolt
Plunging, storming down,
Then disappearing into a rippling pool.

I can almost feel I'm there
Gushing down so scared
It's spraying so much
The energy toppling down
It's roaring in my ears then falling to the ground.

When it finally gets down
I see it frothing up
But as it gets further away
Further away from where it falls
It whispers to me
So calm, so silent, so beautiful
The water is so still.

Sophie Comber (8)
St Catherine's Junior School, Bramley

Waterfalls

The sparkling river,
Running like diamonds,
Energy running through it
Suddenly faster
Screaming, wailing,
Breaking into pieces,
Silence now,
Silence once more.

Amberley Harrison (8)
St Catherine's Junior School, Bramley

Waterfalls!

Gushing water falling away,
Upon a river below,
Dropping, thundering, roaring down,
It sparkles and sprays and makes a waterfall.

It ripples, it's dangerous and frothing,
It screams and plunges along,
It's leaping and dropping,
It sparkles and sprays and makes a waterfall.

It looks amazing and lively,
It topples and tumbles, splashing and dashing,
Then it falls calm and gentle,
It sparkles and sprays,
And carries along.

Olivia Openshaw (8)
St Catherine's Junior School, Bramley

Waterfall

I see the thundering waves fall,
And the sudden roaring
As it is storming down the wall,
The waves are gathering.

It is pounding like your heart,
It is gushing to get to the other end,
You can feel the energy,
It gets to the end and everything
Is suddenly silent.

Isabel Robson (9)
St Catherine's Junior School, Bramley

WATERFALLS!

Waterfalls, waterfalls crashing down,
Roaring, deafening,
All you can hear
The water gushing on hard rock.

It's sudden storming is amazing,
Spraying you like a splashing elephant,
It starts off as a river then . . .
Crash!

Toppling over the cliff,
Lively it is.
It disappears through the mist,
The energy it gets.

Screaming in your ears,
Hard Rock!
The frothing of the water.

As it comes down, it gets calm,
The ripples of the waterfall,
Fades away.

Megan Burling (9)
St Catherine's Junior School, Bramley

LOVE

Love is golden,
It smells of flowers in the spring,
Love tastes of sherbet tickling your throat,
It sounds like a bird singing a song.
Love feels soft and warm,
Love lives in the land over the rainbow,
And in your heart.

Jessica Martyn (10)
St Catherine's Junior School, Bramley

Waterfall

I can see the crashing of the waves,
Falling down the cliff.
Spraying droplets and gushing water,
Roaring over the edge,
It hits the hard rock and carries on.

It's dangerous and misty for a moment
Nothing can be seen.
But then suddenly it appears,
Crashing down.

It gets to the bottom and ripples around
Making a little pool.
It's calm and gentle it's hardly moving
It's like it's lost its energy.

Lauren Chitty (9)
St Catherine's Junior School, Bramley

Waterfall

As the water plunges down
A calm silent river
Goes to a gushing thundering waterfall
Pushing from rock to rock
Down and down
Toppling over each other,
Roaring down the edges
After it's amazing
Clouds of mist cover the area,
With all the energy splashing down,
From a high point,
Then goes streaming down the river.

Monique Hooley (8)
St Catherine's Junior School, Bramley

My Waterfall

You're flowing through a calm, watery plain,
The current's gushing by,
You feel danger approaching,
A sudden drop and you disappear,
Water flinging over your head.

You disappear with no energy left,
The screaming of hard rock beside you,
The plunging water leaping against you,
You have pain all over you,
You thunder to a halt.

A whisper of wind flying past your ear,
You topple to a slow calm movement.
It's all silent,
The sparkling sea is in sight.

Freya Rowson (8)
St Catherine's Junior School, Bramley

Waterfalls!

The waterfall crashes and dashes down the hard rock
It's thundering with energy
Roaring and storming, a deafening sound
Tumbling down it hits the ground.
It sprays everywhere.
But suddenly, it's calm and silent.
The noise has gone.
Disappearing in the mist.
All is quiet
All is gone.

Lotte Barker-Hahlo (9)
St Catherine's Junior School, Bramley

My Waterfall

I'm standing by a waterfall,
It's roaring as it falls.
I can see it flinging down,
Bash, crash, scream.
Its dangerous and lively energy plunges down,
Screaming and gushing and spraying,
It sparkles like stars in the sky,
It's flinging and leaping at me.
It's pounding at the hard rock,
It's amazing to see,
It's at the bottom now,
It's calm and gentle as can be,
It's rippling and silent.

Sian Allen (9)
St Catherine's Junior School, Bramley

Derrick The Dinosaur

Derrick the Dinosaur always forgot,
No one knew why, no one knew what,
He forgot in the morning to get out of bed,
He forgot what to do, with the brain in his head,
He tied knots in his hankies, but that was no use,
He forgot, he washed them and they all came loose,
Derrick decided to take things in hand,
By joining a college for memories and,
My problems are over, I'm a forget me not,
But he missed the first class because he forgot.

Isobel Jordan (11)
St Catherine's Junior School, Bramley

THE SEA

Deep blue sea,
Shells on your shore
Splosh, splash, splish, crash!
Your waves bash on the rocks.

Deep blue sea,
boats in your bay,
Crack, creak, crack, crash!
A shipwreck off your shore.

Deep blue sea,
Calmly you flow,
Splash, splosh, splatter, crash!
Now great waves break through.

Louise Warner (11)
St Catherine's Junior School, Bramley

WATERFALL!

The water crashes down, leaping around,
The sound roars and gushes,
The water is frothing and dashing down the cliff,
The water sprays the hard rock around it.

It thunders down, its energy is amazing,
At the bottom the water is cauldron like,
It's calm, it's silent,
Then whispering, it gently flows on.

Molly Standen-Jewell (9)
St Catherine's Junior School, Bramley

THE WILLOW TREE

My branches fluttered in the wind,
as graceful as a swan
and the ducks swam past
to fly at last.
The sun it peacefully shone.
The children with a picnic sat playing by the dam
the sheep were in the fields all calm with their lamb.
A soft sweet sound of a melancholy song came singing from the birds
and the currents from the river went merrily with the words.
So my little tree, me, the willow
couldn't remember a time when he had been so happy
for the little tree I know
couldn't really show the happiness he had to me.

Sasha Williamson (11)
St Catherine's Junior School, Bramley

DOGS

Small ones, tall ones,
Big ones, little ones,
Cute ones, cuddly ones,
Fat ones, thin ones,
Which one shall I choose?

Black ones, brown ones,
White ones, pink ones!
Crazy ones, lazy ones,
Sad ones, happy ones,
Which one shall I choose?

Caroline Ashton (11)
St Catherine's Junior School, Bramley

THE HAUNTED HOUSE

I stood outside the Haunted House,
Did I dare to enter?
The windows were smashed
Its garden overgrown.

I walked to the huge oak door
It creaked open although no one was there
I nervously crept in
The door slammed behind me.

I trembled with fear
The eerie suits of armour stood holding spears
Cobwebs hung from the corners
A blanket of dust lay on the floor.

I tried to run for the door
Bats flew around my head
I needed to get out
I ran through the mass of black.

I was out
My heart was pounding
Relieved, I started to run home.

Francesca Palmer (11)
St Catherine's Junior School, Bramley

LOVE

Love is pink and fluffy,
It smells like fields of lavender,
Love tastes like chocolate melting in your mouth,
It sounds like the sweet song of a nightingale,
Love feels like a big teddy bear,
Love lives in your heart.

Monica Leaver (11)
St Catherine's Junior School, Bramley

'Twas Midnight

'Twas midnight in the garden,
As Mr Claus flew by,
He slid right down the chimney,
And had a crisp mince pie.

He had a sip of whisky,
A munch of Rudolph's carrot,
And crept upstairs to deliver
A brand new yellow parrot.

Unfortunately the child awoke,
And Mr Claus arose,
He flew off in a jet of smoke,
And gave Rudolph a stroke.

Harriet Mead (10)
St Catherine's Junior School, Bramley

I Need A Hug

I waddled up to my food bowl,
Staring up at the round crisp roll.
I whined and whimpered at the house,
I was so hungry, I could have eaten a mouse.

I walked around the carpet red,
I wanted a hug and a scratch on the head.
I gave a yawn and had a stretch,
I needed a good old game of fetch.

Then the car pulled into the drive,
At least I thought I was still alive.
I ran and jumped up to the mum,
Now I could have some real fun.

Emma Williamson (11)
St Catherine's Junior School, Bramley

BEDD GELERT

Llewelyn left his faithful hound,
Onto his horse he leapt,
Away he rode, he's hunting bound,
But bonny babe, he slept.

A wolf crept in, his fur like sable,
And Gelert sniffed and growled.
So then they fought around the cradle,
The wolf got hurt and howled.

Then Gelert gave wolf such a thud,
And wolf he fell down dead,
Dog looked around, walls stained with blood,
And blankets, babe and bed.

When Llewelyn returned from hunting,
Saw Gelert's snout in gore,
No sign of Baby Bunting,
He struck dog to the floor.

Movements in the blanket stirred
The baby crawled right out.
Then the Lord saw wolf's eyes blurred
As baby smiled with pout.

But poor Gelert lay there dead
Llewelyn did moan and weep.
For he had struck the poor dog's head,
That lay silent in the deepest sleep.

Katherine Young (10)
St Catherine's Junior School, Bramley

My New Puppy

Today's the day
I can't wait.
I am getting it today
I can't wait.
What shall I call it?
I can't wait.
I get in the car
I can't wait.
We drive in silence
I can't wait.
I get out of the car
I can't wait.
I walk through the door
I can't wait.
They are all in a basket
I can't wait.
Which one to pick?
I can't wait.
I'll have that one
I can't wait.
I have my own
I have my own puppy
Worth its wait in gold!

Kirsty Hart (10)
St Catherine's Junior School, Bramley

MAD HAIR DAY!

It's Mad Hair Day,
Everyone looks cool,
As we wander into school,
Everyone stares,
Everyone glares,
And quite a few people are wearing flares.

It's Mad Hair Day,
It's nice and sunny,
And even the teachers are dressed up funny,
We all enjoy as the day progresses,
And only a few people are wearing dresses,
It has been a fantastic way
To spend our Comic Relief Mad Hair Day!

Jennifer Guttridge (10)
St Catherine's Junior School, Bramley

HALLOWE'EN MADNESS

Crumbling walls and dusty gates,
On the walls lie spooky shapes.
My heart is beating out of time,
It sends a shiver down my spine,
As ghostly calls fill the air,
I try to act without a care.

A little girl cries in a corner,
Tears dropping down with great sadness.
I yell, 'Oh help, it's Hallowe'en madness!'

Olivia Biancardi (10)
St Catherine's Junior School, Bramley

Under The Sea?

What's under the sea?
Where I would like to be.
Is it dark and scary
Or full of fish-fairies?
What's under the sea?

What's under the sea?
Is there gold left for me?
Are there jewels which glitter and sparkle?
Are there caves as black as charcoal?
What's under the sea?

What's under the sea?
Are there mermaids laughing with glee?
Do they play all day long
Playing mermaid love songs?
What's under the sea?

Emily Batcheler (10)
St Catherine's Junior School, Bramley

Down Here In This Well

I have been stuck down here in this well for a night and a day.
God has left me here to stay.
All cold and scared I feel betrayed.
Why has he done this?
This is how I have been paid.

Lara Dunlop (11)
St Catherine's Junior School, Bramley

THE DAY MY TEACHER TOOK HER HAIR OFF

That day was normal,
The same as any,
My teacher was dressed formal,
In English we wrote many.

My teacher with hair
All brown and curly,
A red streak with flair,
Some bits all whirly.

Suddenly ripping at this bundle,
She revealed a shiny surface,
The class all grumbled,
'Putting it back on
Would certainly not go amiss, Miss.'

Stephanie Wright (11)
St Catherine's Junior School, Bramley

HEAVENLY HOLIDAYS

There was an angel from Heaven,
Who went to live in Devon.
Met up with the Devil
Whose minions were several,
The chief flew her straight back to Heaven!

Sian Banks (11)
St Catherine's Junior School, Bramley

Night Air

Night air, night air
Beware, beware,
Owls screeching
Robber creeping
Moon shining down.

Night air, night air,
Beware, beware,
Wolf howling,
Fox prowling,
Moon shining down.

Night air, night air,
Beware, beware,
Lost girl,
Stolen pearls,
Moon shining down.

Night air, night air,
Beware, beware,
Begging tramp
Off goes lamp
Moon shining down.

Night air, night air
Beware, beware
Piercing, scream,
Who could it be?
Silence all around!

Maisie Borrows (11)
St Catherine's Junior School, Bramley

The Weather

The sun was shining brightly
The wind was blowing freely
The snow was falling silently
The rain was dropping heavily.

All in one day
How can this happen
We are in England,
It happens!

The hail was heavy when it touched the ground
The ice was loud when it fell from the sky
The clouds were light when they covered the sun
A rainbow formed arching high and far.

All in one day
How can this happen
We are in England
It happens!

Sarah Taylor (10)
St Catherine's Junior School, Bramley

STEALING FROM A SWEET SHOP

Shelves above,
They look so tempting
Chocolate, sweets and jars of lollipops
Honeycones and pots of liquorice.

I'll eat a sweet and then another
More and more, my tummy's rumbling.
Heart's pumping faster
What if I'm caught?
I'll spend my life completing chores.

Get out a bag, fill it with sweets
Rainbow drops, sherbet lemons,
Chocolate fudge and runny toffee
Doesn't sound so very yummy.

Out the window
Footsteps are coming
But I carry on running
Running away from my fate.

Annabel Pettit (10)
St Catherine's Junior School, Bramley

Sweets

Red ones
Orange ones
Blue ones
Green ones
Which one shall I pick?

Sweet ones,
Sour ones,
Sticky ones,
Smooth ones,
Which one shall I pick?

Ones to chew
Ones to suck
Ones to refresh
Ones to smell
Which one shall I pick?

Ones with wrappers
Ones on their own
Ones in packets
Ones in bags
Which one shall I pick?

Liberty Saunders (11)
St Catherine's Junior School, Bramley

Casper

I have a big black hairy pet,
Casper is his name,
Sometimes he gets soaking wet,
But he thinks it's a game.

He always likes to play outdoors,
Especially in the park,
He comes inside with muddy paws,
He also likes to bark.

Casper sniffs things with his nose,
He loves to run and play,
It tickles when he licks my toes,
He's my doggy, by the way.

Alice Miller (9)
St Dunstan's CE Primary School, Sutton

One Day I Met A Dog

One day I met a dog,
A nice dog,
A cheeky dog,
A friendly dog,
A fast dog,
A fat dog,
A golden dog,
A muddy dog,
A happy dog,
A lovely dog,
And his name was Chip.

Lindsay Geoghegan (8)
St Dunstan's CE Primary School, Sutton

THE SNOWMAN GROWS

As I looked out of my window
One frosty morning while my parents
Were dozing and snoring
I saw the whole world had turned sparkling white,
I gasped with joy, what an astonishing sight.

I threw on my clothes wrapped up
For the snow
Ran down the stairs getting ready to go
Running to the door,
Boots, gloves, hat and scarf
Out in the garden
Trying to find the path.

Piling up the snow,
Making it into a ball,
One big one small it was getting tall.

Eyes of coal with a carrot nose,
Twigs for arms,
A smiling mouth, I suppose.

The snowman was finished,
What could I do?

'Come in' says Mum,
'I've got breakfast for you.'

James Occomore (8)
St Dunstan's CE Primary School, Sutton

Billy's Coming Back

The word is on the street: Billy's coming back,
Teachers are groaning,
Kids are hiding,
Now that Billy's coming back.

Policemen are legging it,
Lockers are being locked,
Secret bases are being evacuated,
Now that Billy's coming back.

It was so wonderful when he left
For a military school in Canada,
Three years later, it's all been spoilt,
Now that Billy's coming back.

Sweets are being hidden,
Chocolate is being scoffed,
The Star Trek fans are bailing out,
Now that Billy's coming back.

So look for a figure in a purple jacket,
Walking down the road,
If he looks like he's looking for a fight,
It's probably Billy coming back.

Please don't try to stop him,
Give him what he wants,
You can't do anything fun now,
Cause Billy's coming back.

So bar up all your windows,
Lock the garden door,
The mayor doesn't run this town anymore,
Now that Billy's coming back.

Thomas Blagden (11)
St Dunstan's CE Primary School, Sutton

A Spell To Banish War

Get lost war,
Get back to where you belong!

Get back to the valley of death,
And I hope you stay there long.

Get lost war,
Get back to where you belong!

How dare you kill my country,
How dare you bring sorrow and pain.

Vamoose war!
Peace has invaded our country
So you are not welcome anymore.

Get back to the valley of death,
Go and never return!

Laura Brady (10)
St Dunstan's CE Primary School, Sutton

War

War smells of sweaty men,
It tastes of sour lemons,
It feels as sharp as a sword,
It sounds like people dying,
It looks like Hell,
War is Satan's language.

Claire Raftery (10)
St Dunstan's CE Primary School, Sutton

EMOTIONS

Happiness is the colour of yellow
It smells like warm crusty baked bread
Happiness tastes like melted cream chocolate
It sounds like 1000 white doves singing a tuneful song
Happiness feels warm and cuddly
It lives right down in my passionate heart!

Anger is the colour of blood
It smells of rotting decay
Anger tastes burnt and bitter
It sounds like a volcano steaming and bubbling,
Anger feels scorching hot
It lives in bad tempered people!

Dominque Havelock-Hill (9)
St Dunstan's CE Primary School, Sutton

SUMMER SUN

Summer has a golden face,
With bright fiery robes.
Summer has a joyful smile,
And loves to come out and play.
Summer lives on the sun,
Watching over the planets.
Summer brings a smile,
To everybody's face.
Summer smells of sweet roses,
Swaying in the breeze,
Summer is a kind and happy person,
Which loves to come each day.

Adam Heasman (11)
St Dunstan's CE Primary School, Sutton

THE GORILLA'S PLEA

The rainforest is our home,
The tree's our golden throne.

Then you come to chop down trees to sell,
And make our lives plain hell.

You are related to us,
So why are you doing this to us?

We don't hurt mankind
And now we're hard to find.

We're all dying out - every one,
Something must be done.

Please help, please do,
Someone can change things - maybe it's *you!*

Jocelyn Amer (10)
St Dunstan's CE Primary School, Sutton

ON THE TIP TOP TICK

(Based on 'On The Ning Nang Nong' by Spike Milligan)

On the tip top tick
When the pigs say flick
And the birds just chirp in the trees,
For the cats and the dogs
And the mice and the hogs
Dance round with the bugs and the fleas,
On the tip top tick.

Kirsty Macphie (9)
St Dunstan's CE Primary School, Sutton

The School Sound Collector

(Based on 'The Sound Collector' by Roger McGough)

A stranger called this morning
Dressed all in black and grey,
Put every sound into a bay
And carried them away.

The moaning of the teacher
The ticking of the clock
The tearing of the paper
The ripping of a frock.

The scribbling of pencils,
The chewing of the gum
The whispering of the kids
A mouse eating a crumb.

The crying of the kids
The knocking on doors
The flushing of the loos
The squeaking of saws.

The typing of computers
The banging of a drum
The writing of pencils
While doing a maths sum.

A stranger called this morning
He didn't leave his name
Left us only silence
School will never be the same.

Samantha Williams (11)
St Dunstan's CE Primary School, Sutton

A Spell To Banish Wrinkles

Go away wrinkles
You're ruining my skin.

Why don't you bug someone else,
Someone like the King?

Go away wrinkles,
You are my complication.

I try and try for you to go away,
I even use foundation!

My skin was soft before you came,
So please, please
Go away!

Isobel Ford (10)
St Dunstan's CE Primary School, Sutton

A Spell To Banish . . . Hate

Go away hate and never come back
You're the one who needs a good old whack.

Go away hate and stay where you go,
You've hurt more people than I will ever know.

Go away hate you're a ball of flames,
You always call people, horrid, horrid names.

Go away hate you're not wanted here,
You're the one who needs a slap round the ear.

Go away hate if you think you're smart,
You have broken lots of people's hearts.

Sophie Penwarden (10)
St Dunstan's CE Primary School, Sutton

THE SILENT MAN

(Based on 'The Sound Collector' by Roger McGough)

Peter Piper came today
Dressed in white and black,
He put the sounds in his bag
And placed it in his hat.

The moaning of the children
The scraping of the chalk,
The running of the corridor
The talking came to naught.

The flushing of the toilets,
The whinging of the teacher
The fussing of the children
Killing every creature.

The smacking of the ruler
The kicking of the ball
The crying of the girls
The music in the hall.

The rattling of the trays
The ticking of the clocks
The hitting of the bullies,
Even the rustle of the fox.

The clashing of the cutlery
The ringing of the bell
The screeching in the playground
The banging when they fell.

Peter Piper turned up this morning
He didn't bare his age
Left us only silence
Life will never be the same.

Jack Carter (11)
St Dunstan's CE Primary School, Sutton

WINTER'S HERE

Winter's here,
Blowing into the city,
Pushing people through,
Which makes such a pity,
Shouting into the winter walls.

Children wearing furry clothes,
Winter's jealousy has begun,
Sending messages to his feet,
To stamp and kill them,
Who can retreat?

Blustering noises from the mouth,
Pulling the thick ice to the ground,
Making his slaves plough roads,
Loads of people all not found.

The news breaks out
On the television,
Thousands killed,
By the winter's snow.

Jamie Crawford (11)
St Dunstan's CE Primary School, Sutton

JEALOUSY

Go away jealousy
I can't count how many people you've made hate each other
How many people you've given a sour feeling to.

Go back to Hell or the place you come from
Don't come near me jealousy
I've had enough of you
Go away.

Henry Burke (10)
St Dunstan's CE Primary School, Sutton

THE CLASSROOM OF DEATH

Creak goes the wooden door,
Tip toe once inside.
Dust deserts the hollow walls,
As the hand receives the sides.

The crying of the children,
The praying of the dying,
As double maths homework,
Strikes by spying.

The pleading of the desperate,
Is always never heard,
As it is isolated,
From any other being.

Michael Swain (10)
St Dunstan's CE Primary School, Sutton

A SPELL TO BANISH WINTER

Go away winter,
How dare you cover everything with ice?
Go away winter, and never come back.
Stop waving your wand of condensation.
Go away winter, and never come back,
Stop steaming up our windows.
Go away winter, and never come back.
Stop giving people colds and coughs,
Go away winter, and never come back,
Oh I wish you could just melt away.

Elizabeth Peck (11)
St Dunstan's CE Primary School, Sutton

THE SCHOOL

The boarding school comes nearer,
The gates they open wide,
It's the starting of an era
Of my isolation inside.

Cut off from people short and long,
With every last hope gone.
My homework mighty and strong,
For I'm the only one.

Nobody to talk to
No one to care
When you stub your toe,
In the corner over there.

I made that bit up, so don't dare worry
I'm perfectly normal, just in a hurry!

Sophie Dix (10)
St Dunstan's CE Primary School, Sutton

A SPELL TO BANISH EXAMS, TESTS AND TEACHERS

Q1 Go back test. Stay away you drain fun out of kids.
Q2 I hate you exam, so why do you test us children?
Q3 I wish you would go back to teachers and give them a hard time.
Q4 You are so evil, you give kids papercuts and exhausted brains.
Q5 You think you're so clever, but you're not, you're only a piece of paper.
Q6 Get packing and take the train to the shredder.
Q7 I am going to get rid of you once and for all.

James Tonge (10)
St Dunstan's CE Primary School, Sutton

Spell To Banish Braces

Go away braces,
Go back to the dentist.

Go take a long walk off a short pier
And never come back again.

Go away braces,
Go back to the dentist.

How dare you fit in my mouth
You make me lisp.

I don't want you here,
I always have to take you out.

Go away braces,
Go back to the dentist.

I would rather run into a wall,
Than have you in my mouth.

If only life was that simple.

Archie Cork (10)
St Dunstan's CE Primary School, Sutton

Friendships

Friendships last forever
Friendships never break
Friendships stick together
Friendships comfort you
Friendships come first
Friendships are always together.

Zoe Pullen (10)
St Dunstan's CE Primary School, Sutton

CATCH THAT PUP

3, 2, 1 catch that pup

Megan's running down the stairs!
Alex is sprinting on the landing!
Fudge is hiding in the basement!
It's neck 'n' neck.
Then crash the dustbin falls over
Back on track.
It's Megan!
It's Alex!
Alex is zooming round the corners
Oh no, Fudge is on the trampoline.
Alex following!
Megan catching up!
Owe, Ee, ooo
Banging heads!
The pup's back inside!
'Catch that dog!'
'Mum, stop interfering!
Fudge has got my toy.'
'Dad!'
'Wait, stop the race!'
'Alex stop crying!'
(Mum and Dad join the race)
'Get that pup!'
Punching, kicking, grabbing, shoving!
'Mum, that hurt.'
'Yes, Dad has got the dog.'
'Oh no Alex's toy!'

Megan Douglas (10)
St Dunstan's CE Primary School, Sutton

A Spell To Banish Teachers

Take a hike teachers
No one wants you here.

Take a hike teachers,
You all should take a long walk off a short pier.

Get away French teacher!
'Scuse me, sil vous plait you're really not here to stay.

Get away DT teacher,
I think your brain is made of clay.

Move it maths teacher!
We already know how to count to three.

Move it English teacher
You need to learn your ABCs.

I banish you to oblivion!
You should let us chat.

If only life was as easy as . . .
    that.

Alex Lathbridge (10)
St Dunstan's CE Primary School, Sutton

Twinkle Twinkle Little Bow

Twinkle twinkle little bow,
Play this fast, then play it slow.
Draw your bow across the string,
Careful not to make it *ping!*

Connie Pullen (8)
St Dunstan's CE Primary School, Sutton

The Spell To Banish Homework

Do not give us homework
Please, please, please.

Go away homework
Get back where you belong.

Buzz off homework
To where your planet is.

Do not give us homework
Please, please, please.

Mind your own business,
I've got other things to do.

Why do you come?
I hate you, just drop dead.

Do not give us homework
Please, please, *please*
Just go away!

Ella Pennyfather (10)
St Dunstan's CE Primary School, Sutton

There Was A Girl Called Lin

There was a girl called Lin
Who poked herself with a pin
She played with her dog
Then kissed a frog
And she was very thin.

Savannah Worne (8)
St Dunstan's CE Primary School, Sutton

MY DOG DAISY

I would love to have a dog
One day my mother said to me.
I will love to have one anyway.
And she came to stay.

She seemed a part of the family now
She runs with me and plays
We snuggle in bed together
At the end of happy days.

Rebecca Barham (8)
St Dunstan's CE Primary School, Sutton

WHAT CAN I WRITE MY STORY ABOUT?

What can I write my story about?
A rat, a toad, a pig's snout?
Do you know I'm not quite sure?
Maybe a rusty door?
Or maybe a cricket match?
Or maybe a chicken trying to hatch?
None of those seem good enough,
It's making my life very tough.
I've got it! I won't write a story,
They're too gory.
I'll write a poem,
The one I've just done.
The one I've just done,
Shall be the one.

Abigail Foster (10)
St Hilary's School, Godalming

A Day To Remember

I stand on the shore and watch the surfers go by,
And the seagulls swooping low
And boys jumping off rocks very high
And the Punch and Judy Show.

I stand on the shore and touch the soft sand,
Then the rough and jagged rocks,
Then I feel the lapping waves as I stand,
Then the breeze on my face and locks.

I stand on the shore and hear the shouts of children playing
And the pounding of the waves,
And the barks of dogs straying,
And the echoes from the caves.

I stand on the shore and smell the salt in the air
The smell of fish grilling,
The smoky curls from the flames that glare,
The air these scents are filling.

I stand on the shore and taste my ice cream,
It is a strawberry flavour.
It is all better than a dream,
It is a day to savour.

Mary Tyler (10)
St Hilary's School, Godalming

DREAMS

I had a terrible dream once,
In the forest quite alone quite alone
There appeared from nowhere
Goblins, witches throwing me out from my home.

I had an unbelievable dream
I went through this amazing dimension
Sparkly bubbles everywhere
Fairies dancing to the music, floating in suspension.

I had a nothing dream I guess
Though sad to see someone go
I then woke up with a terrible bump
And all the dreams went a-flow.

Jenny North (10)
St Hilary's School, Godalming

THE TIMETABLE

First it's boring maths
Then it's horrible music
Afterwards it's double science
Then of *course* it's break.

After break it's horrid history
And then stinky French
After that it's not too bad
Because it's English with Mrs Colgon.

At 4 o'clock time for art
With Mrs Knapp and Mrs Farr
Then I change to dance mode
At last it's time to go home.

Katherine Bodie (9)
St Hilary's School, Godalming

WATERFALLS

Glistening, sparkling waterfalls,
Hidden in a cave, in the deep of the dark.
A waterfall awaits you, it's waiting for you.
You cross a bridge, it feels strange though.
You hear exotic sounds, you enter afraid quietly.
The sound's getting louder, it's getting very suspicious
There's a boat waiting for you, a flute is playing in the backyard.
You get in the boat, the water is very raw, somehow.
A bird floats over the surface of the water singing its tune,
The paradise has come, nature is with you in the cave.
The song is familiar, you follow the bird.
It leads to a pathway, you follow the path.
Birds are singing merrily, feeding their young.
A waterfall awaits you. Paradise is
Here with you.

Philippa Goff (10)
St Hilary's School, Godalming

CHOCOLATE

C hocolate, plain, milk or white,
H as your mouth watering at the sight.
O range, mint or strawberry cream,
C an carry you off in a delightful dream.
O r nuts like Brazil or hazel.
L ovely caramel, toffee or fudge,
A ttacks your mouth with a dreadful smudge.
T errible if you cannot eat,
E at this wonderful tasty treat.

Charlotte Horne (9)
St Hilary's School, Godalming

The Garden

As I step into the divine garden,
the fragrance is so sweet and tender.
Little dewdrops just like crystals,
kiss the graceful flowers.

As I turn around,
beautiful bluebells cover the ground,
as they sway in the cooling shade
of a blossoming apple tree.

Passion fruits grow up tall,
but by far the most beautiful of them all.
Is the rose the wonderful rose.

As the rose petals unfurl,
in a delicate way all the petals curl.
As it unfolds its magic pattern
not one of those precious petals are flattened.

As I step out of the garden
the beautiful fragrance is still with me.
Little dewdrops just like crystals
kiss the graceful flowers.

Alexandra Stevens (10)
St Hilary's School, Godalming

I Am Not All Bad

I might be a menace,
I might be a pain,
I might always be the same,
But still you should cope with me,
I'm not all bad,
You never know I might make you glad.

Hannah Robertson (10)
St Hilary's School, Godalming

FIONA THE FLIRT

Fiona the flirt she flirts with boys
Fiona the flirt she flirts with her toys.
Fiona the flirt she flirts in class
And when the teacher asks her a question, she always says 'Pass.'
Her friends and she are triple trouble
And when they're together she flirts double!
When she goes to pop concerts, with her mates,
They all shout *'Gareth Gates!'*
And when it's Will Young
She sticks out her tongue.
When she gets home she takes off her flirting skirt,
And that's about all of *Fiona the Flirt.*

Rebecca Rowe (10)
St Hilary's School, Godalming

FRIENDS

F is for fun which we always have.
R is for racing which we do in the playground.
I is for the game 'It' which me and my friends play.
E is for education which we do at school.
N is for naughty which I never am.
D is for DT a subject we do at school.
S is for my best friend ever Sofia.

Kylie Pang (9)
St Hilary's School, Godalming

INSPIRED BY THE FIRE OF LONDON

It silently stalked around the streets
Creeping through narrow gaps
As if a miraculous monster, devouring strong
Proud and erect with upright head.

Fiona Travers (10)
St James The Great RC Primary School, Thornton Heath

INSPIRED BY THE FIRE OF LONDON

The flames hungrily strode, becoming more ferocious by the hour,
The blaze stroking the compass points of London,
People scampering out of their no longer standing houses,
Devastated dreamers drown all life and thought.

Catherine Hickland (10)
St James The Great RC Primary School, Thornton Heath

INSPIRED BY THE FIRE OF LONDON

The fire, blazing along the criss-cross streets,
To either side his fiery wings he spreads,
Engulfing mean houses in its path,
And leaves the great old city in shreds.

Philippa James (9)
St James The Great RC Primary School, Thornton Heath

Inspired By The Fire Of London

Now, the king wakes up with a sound
Of people crying all around
The houses spitting the sound of fire
The flames rising higher and higher.

Holly McDonagh (10)
St James The Great RC Primary School, Thornton Heath

Inspired By The Fire Of London

Nothing stops the monster from the depths of Hell
The flamed forked tongues lick round another prey
Wealthy houses grow a ghastly red array
The gaping red mouth swallows a larger kill.

Rachel Ivens (9)
St James The Great RC Primary School, Thornton Heath

Inspired By The Fire Of London

Woken by the sounds of dying,
Their distant calls are heard aloud
People fleeing from the crying,
Pushing past the running crowd.

Zoë Faircloth (10)
St James The Great RC Primary School, Thornton Heath

INSPIRED BY THE FIRE OF LONDON

No help avails, as the grotesque monstrous beast,
Sweeps through the murky London streets.
Before the rich are comfortable in their beds,
The hot breath of the monster devours them.

Joanna D'Cruz (10)
St James The Great RC Primary School, Thornton Heath

INSPIRED BY THE FIRE OF LONDON

The ferocious fire meanwhile strides around,
To either palm his wings he stretches out
He darts the streets and engulfs everything in his path,
His fiery claws reached th'other side.

Hannah Cobb (9)
St James The Great RC Primary School, Thornton Heath

INSPIRED BY THE FIRE OF LONDON

The streets become crowded and lively like daytime,
People scurry with buckets to get water from the precious well,
People dissect water pipes, and others approach in the engines,
And some brave people climb ladders as the fire burns.

Becky McGowan (9)
St James The Great RC Primary School, Thornton Heath

Inspired By The Fire Of London

A blaze of flares stretched all along the Thames
And illuminated the flowing water with its outburst
The ruffled waves thundered, engulfing the flames
And bewildered fish swam furiously for breath.

Nicole Mascarenhas (10)
St James The Great RC Primary School, Thornton Heath

Inspired By The Fire Of London

Now in a small enclosed space it quietly tiptoed,
Slowly scorching, travelling, burning timber:
This evil giant, engulfing all in its path,
Strolled bravely with no fuss.

Aishling Bennett (9)
St James The Great RC Primary School, Thornton Heath

Inspired By The Fire Of London

The fire is a roaring lion, it's huge,
It's getting bigger and bigger as it goes,
It's melting buildings and killing children,
The flames are unstoppable as they clasp the houses.

Francesca Ferrari (10)
St James The Great RC Primary School, Thornton Heath

Inspired By The Fire Of London

A thunderball of fire shot along the bank,
And shone along the water with its fearsome flames.
The churning waves charging like army tanks,
And flitting fish swam swiftly to safety.

Lauren Waldron (9)
St James The Great RC Primary School, Thornton Heath

Reflections On The Fire Of London

A steaming flame of fire raced
Along the river's bank,
And brightened roaring waves.
People jumped in the water,
But down they sank,
The rest were taken over by
The fire and became helpless slaves.

Georgia Jasper (9)
St James The Great RC Primary School, Thornton Heath

Inspired By The Fire Of London

Then in quiet still it sneaked along,
The room demolished in burning wings,
Grown from a few to an army of flames,
Fighting furiously, fated to win.

Rachel Humphries (10)
St James The Great RC Primary School, Thornton Heath

LIGHTNING

The lightning
    Flashing
Blinding bright,
    Sounds of crashing
All through the night.
    Girls and boys
In their beds
    Sleepless nights are ahead.

Lauren Byrne (9)
St James The Great RC Primary School, Thornton Heath

INSPIRED BY THE FIRE OF LONDON

The streets were crowded and got busy and more,
Brave ones ran for the water to really try,
So many were frightened at what they saw,
Burning and scorching with children's awful cry.

Roisin Kelly (10)
St James The Great RC Primary School, Thornton Heath

INSPIRED BY THE FIRE OF LONDON

The colossal flames dart to the houses,
Panic engulfing, no thought for their clothes,
Mothers start howling as realisation dawns,
Their babies are left among the flames from Hell.

Katherine Foad (10)
St James The Great RC Primary School, Thornton Heath

INSPIRED BY THE FIRE OF LONDON

As days, nights go on panic widens:
Men, women shout, 'More water, more water.'
Water pumps, bellowing engines screeching,
The sensible brave fight flames from ladders.

Amy Kavanagh (10)
St James The Great RC Primary School, Thornton Heath

INSPIRED BY THE FIRE OF LONDON

The men as comforting as can be,
While women grieve like rivers fled,
As they strike abreast too late,
Knowing they cannot do anything but watch the
Flame murderer kill their precious.

Michaela Newsome (9)
St James The Great RC Primary School, Thornton Heath

INSPIRED BY THE FIRE OF LONDON

The tower of flames does not cease or go out,
A devil engulfing our entire race.
He patrols the streets, his arms strong and stout,
And in a boat on the river, smoke is what poor souls taste.

James Diffley (9)
St James The Great RC Primary School, Thornton Heath

INSPIRED BY THE FIRE OF LONDON

Now the sun rises, noise wakes the king,
His rightful duty has stolen him from rest.
Message for the king the servants bring,
'Beware the fire,' the uninvited guest.

Christian Leggett (9)
St James The Great RC Primary School, Thornton Heath

INSPIRED BY THE FIRE OF LONDON

The lucky ones, stand in the field
Staring at the ashes that once were their homes
And replaying the screams of their children burning to death in their heads, and some watching
Upon the wet field their children sleep.

Sorcha Nestor (10)
St James The Great RC Primary School, Thornton Heath

THE HUGE OAK HAIKU

The huge oak stands tall,
With its strong roots under me
It will never fall.

Sarah Day (9)
St Peter's CE (Aided) Primary School, Farnham

Cheetah Began

For his run,
He stole the speed of a rocket
He stole the legs of an Olympic runner
He stole the speed of lightning.

For his teeth,
He stole the teeth of a walrus
He stole the point from a hunting knife.

For his tail
He stole the wagging of a donkey's tail
He stole the length of a walking stick.

For his spots,
He stole the spots of a giant ladybird
He stole the black of a black sky.

For his coat,
He stole the colour of the sun
He stole lava from a volcano,
He stole the feel of a bit of fur.

To make the cheetah.

Ben Jeggo (10)
St Peter's CE (Aided) Primary School, Farnham

The Shark

It swims all day and its teeth are very sharp,
Some sharks are as gentle as a harp.

They can smell blood for miles,
Meat in its tummy is stored in piles,
Their teeth are lots of giant files.

Charlie Trenholm (9)
St Peter's CE (Aided) Primary School, Farnham

CHEETAH BEGAN

Cheetah began . . .

For his run . . .
He stole the speed of light,
He stole the power of a rocket,
He stole the strength of a boxer.

For his teeth . . .
He stole the redness of a used dagger,
He stole the shape of an icicle
He stole the sharpness of the elephant's tusks.

For his coat . . .
He stole the blackness of a burnt sausage,
He stole the yellow of the ray from the sun,
And made his soft, spotty coat.

For his eyes . . .
He stole the pitch-black of ink,
He stole the glowing of a firefly
He stole the darkness of a starless night.

Finally he was made.

James Cooles (10)
St Peter's CE (Aided) Primary School, Farnham

MY BUNNY

My bunny, oh my bunny
Is so funny, oh is so funny.
She looks so gold, oh so gold.
She's never cold, oh never cold.
She's worth lots of money, oh lots of money.
Because she's my bunny, oh my bunny!

Daisy Meyer (8)
St Peter's CE (Aided) Primary School, Farnham

DOLPHIN BEGAN

For her skin . . .
She snatched the smoothness of silk
She snatched the grey of an elephant.

She snatched the end of a long balloon
She snatched the roundness of a ball
To make her nose.

For her fin . . .
She snatched the hook of a coathanger
She snatched the feel of varnished wood.

She snatched the moving of a see-saw
She snatched the letter Y from the alphabet
For her tail.

For her voice . . .
She snatched the creaking of an old door
She snatched the noise of an injured eagle
And dolphin was made.

Amy Rice (10)
St Peter's CE (Aided) Primary School, Farnham

TIGERS

Tigers waiting in bushes ready to pounce.
Hunting animals all day.
Nothing will stop them or get in their way.
They claw and they tear, they hunt and kill.
They have razor-sharp claws coming out of their paws.

Thomas Graham (8)
St Peter's CE (Aided) Primary School, Farnham

Happiness

Happiness is talking to your mum and dad.
Happiness is having friends.
Happiness is being kind.
Happiness is getting pocket money.
Happiness is going home.
Happiness is not getting bullied.
Happiness is playing football.
Happiness is going to school.
Happiness is seeing your friends.
Happiness is spreading peace around.

Jamie Clements (10)
St Peter's CE (Aided) Primary School, Farnham

The Starfish

There is a starfish in the sea,
Floating by right next to me.

The starfish floated onto the shore,
I gave him seaweed, he wanted more.

I couldn't figure out what to do,
He'd slipped into my shoe.

There is a starfish in the sea
Floating by right next to me.

Sophie Seekings (9)
St Peter's CE (Aided) Primary School, Farnham

MOUSE BEGAN

He stole the sleekness of silk,
He stole the shining of a new coin,
He stole the thinness of a sheet of paper,
And his coat was made.

He stole the length of a piece of string,
He stole the thickness of a piece of hair,
He stole the pink of a pig's snout,
And his tail was made.

He stole the twitching of a rabbit's nose,
He stole the shape of a piece of thin wire,
He stole the long bristles from a man's beard,
And his whiskers were made.

He stole the feel of a potato peel,
He stole the shape of a shell,
He stole the softness of a newborn baby's skin,
And his ears were made.

He stole the smallest apple pip,
He stole the cold of a wet pebble,
He stole the black of a dirty hand,
And his nose was made.

Finally mouse was made.

Francesca Williams (11)
St Peter's CE (Aided) Primary School, Farnham

Scorpion Began

For his tail . . .
He stole the point of a dagger
He stole the prick of a pin
He stole the kill of an arrow.

For his eyes . . .
He stole the darkness of the night sky
He stole the reflection of a mirror
He stole the black of death.

For his claws . . .
He stole the crushing grip of a python
He stole the crescent moon's sleek curve
He stole the sharp spikes of Hell.

For his legs . . .
He stole the sun's curve
He stole the six pikemen's spears
He stole the sharpness of swords.

For his skin . . .
He stoke the blackness of a crypt
He stole the hairs of an unshaven man
He stole the darkness of shadow.

William Beattie (10)
St Peter's CE (Aided) Primary School, Farnham

Peace

I like to have peace with a horse and a hamster
And a cat because they are soft and nice and cuddly
My horse is a big big nice horse and I like animals
And I want peace with all animals and God and Jesus.

Lesley Green (8)
St Peter's CE (Aided) Primary School, Farnham

Polar Bear Began

Polar bear began
He took the unguarded depth from a whale,
He took the unguarded swiftness of the wind,
For his swim.

He took the unguarded texture of leather gloves
He took the unguarded size of comical slippers,
For his feet.

From deep forests,
He took the unguarded caution of a deer
He took the unguarded silence of the leaves on the trees
For his walk.

For his eyes . . .
He took the glistening of pebbles
And for their shape
He took the unguarded raisins.

For his fur coat
He took the unguarded fluffiness of a cloud,
He took the unguarded whiteness of snow
    And polar bear was made.

Rachel Marriott (11)
St Peter's CE (Aided) Primary School, Farnham

Caterpillar Crawls - Haiku

Caterpillar crawls
Crawls towards the cabbage patch
Caterpillar crawls!

Jamie Crawford (9)
St Peter's CE (Aided) Primary School, Farnham

THE MONKEY

I was walking through the forest to see what I could see,
A great big monkey staring at me.

It jumped up and started to swing,
It looked like a silly furry thing.

The monkey came jumping down the tree,
It was jumping on my hurt left knee.

The monkey sat down and started to talk,
'Hello' he said 'Why don't we go for a walk?'

I jumped up in shock,
Right out of my yellow frilly frock.

I got up and started to run,
Come to think of it that was quite fun.

I was walking through the forest to see what I could see,
A great big monkey following me.

Rebecca Cooles (8)
St Peter's CE (Aided) Primary School, Farnham

THE ELEPHANT

His big ears help him cool down in the sunlight.
His trunk helps him find food.
His big feet pound the dusty earth when he is in a hurry.
His eyelids close and open as the dust blows back in his big head.
His tail waves like a flag, trying to keep the flies away
And then it's time for an elephant's bath
Their favourite place!

Ella Bennett (9)
St Peter's CE (Aided) Primary School, Farnham

THE LIONS' CAVE

The lions' cave is wet and damp and dark
The lions can sleep all day and night,
The females go to hunt and catch a zebra
The lions eat and eat and the cubs too.
Males first, then the rest,
Say *roar*, say *zzz*, say *purr*.

Their cubs are so cute they love to play nearly all day,
There is only one father in one pride,
So lions are not much different
I wish we could be friends.

Hannah Barratt (8)
St Peter's CE (Aided) Primary School, Farnham

MY DOG

My dog is called Rosie
She has a little friend,
They play together all day long
Having fun,
In the sun
They leap and jump
And roll about,
At the end of the day they say goodbye
And go back home,
They hope to see each other
Another day.

Louise Macnaghten (9)
St Peter's CE (Aided) Primary School, Farnham

WHALE BEGAN

For her tail . . .
She used the shape of a bow
She used the movement of an eel
She used the softness of a squidgy ball.

She used the beadiness of an olive pip
She used the black of the night
She used the size of an ant
And made her eyes.

To make her skin . . .
She used the roughness of a road
She used the wetness of a running stream
She used the darkness of the deepest ocean.

She used the length of a steamer
She used the weight of a few elephants
She used the width of the Albert Hall
And made her stomach.

She used the roughness of sandpaper
She used the pinkness of dawn
She used the width of a mountain
To make her tongue.

And whale was made.

Isabelle Ciechanewicz (10)
St Peter's CE (Aided) Primary School, Farnham

Dog Began

Dog began.

For his ears . . .
He took the sharpness of the eagle's cry
He took the points of a snake's tongue
He took the straightness of the stars.

He took the sound of the underground
He took the growl of the tiger
He took howl of the wolf
To make his voice.

For his eyes . . .
He took the twinkle of the stars
He took the blackness of the night
He took the fog from the sky.

To make his coat . . .
He took the softness of the baby owl
He took the smoothness of a feather
He took the texture of a pine tree

And dog was made.

Rachel Willis (9)
St Peter's CE (Aided) Primary School, Farnham

Peace

I want peace with my family
I want peace with my friend
I want peace in the world
I want peace with all animals
I want peace with all people!

Andrew Jackson (9)
St Peter's CE (Aided) Primary School, Farnham

GERBIL BEGAN

For his teeth he snatched
Pointed thorns from a mature rosebush
Bone coloured needles from a woven box full of wool.

For his eyes he snatched
The darkness of a deserted cave
A dark black reflective marble from a packed toy shop.

For his claws he snatched
The feel of a stinging nettle in a corner of a worn-out field
The roughness of a small dinosaur fossil.

For his fur he snatched
The softness of a candyfloss textured cloud
The fluffiness of a young chick's coat from a chicken's
uncomfortable nest.

For his tail he snatched
The shape of the bright moon from the dark sky
The point of a sharp dagger from a hunting man's old bag
And Gerbil was born.

Charlotte Rogers (10)
St Peter's CE (Aided) Primary School, Farnham

SOPHIE THE DOG

Sophie the dog is a playful dog and loves to play with her ball
One day we went along to the park and she dropped it over the river
bank.
Soon it floated down the river.
And after all that happened sadly we didn't get it and Sophie
Was not happy.
So even though she wasn't happy neither was I a happy chappy!

Jonathan Wright (9)
St Peter's CE (Aided) Primary School, Farnham

Shark Began

For his scales . . .
He stole the fatal cut of coral
He stole the grey of a misty morning
He stole the reflection of light on a mirror.

He stole the perpetual blackness of a miner's tunnel
He stole the size of an ant's abdomen
He stole the haunting look of danger
And made his eyes.

He stole the sharp point of a cruel icicle
He stole the ridges from the Wall of China
He stole the curve of a model's body
And made his tail.

For his manoeuvre . . .
He stole the relaxed saunter of the king around his subjects
He stole the agility from a darting cheetah
He stole the wiggle of a newborn baby.

For his teeth . . .
He stole the colour of warm, old milk
He stole the thorn's evil prick
He stole a fountain pen's daggered point.
And shark was made.

Kate Wilson (11)
St Peter's CE (Aided) Primary School, Farnham

Peace

I would like peace to drop against the Earth
We would like no fighting and be just a peaceful world.
I like the way peace drops against the Earth,
It is like the rain going *drip drop drip drop.*

Emily Marshall (8)
St Peter's CE (Aided) Primary School, Farnham

Horse Began

For her eyes she stole smooth, black pebbles
from the bottom of a rushing river
and children's muddy tennis balls.

She stole the softness of the queen's best soft satin dress,
and the smooth of a sleeping child's duvet
and made her muzzle.

She stole wispy thickness of fuse wire
She stole the texture of hard spaghetti
She stole the movement of opening and closing curtains
And made her tail.

She stole the roughness of a man's beard
And the fluffiness of a young chick
And made her coat.

She stole the speed of an aeroplane taking off
And the sound of the whistling wind
And made her speed.
    Horse was born!

Sophie Paine (11)
St Peter's CE (Aided) Primary School, Farnham

HAMMERHEAD BEGAN

For its skin . . .
He snatched the skin off the back of a pig.
He snatched a massive piece of rubber

For its eyes . . .
He snatched two oranges
He snatched a pot of ink.

For its tail . . .
He snatched a triangle
He snatched the sharp of an electric guitar.

For its head . . .
He snatched a semicircle
He snatched the letter T.

For its teeth . . .
He snatched a butcher's knife
He snatched a sharp rock

Hammerhead was made.

Ben Bishop (10)
St Peter's CE (Aided) Primary School, Farnham

SPIDER BEGAN

For his hair . . .
He grabbed the bristles of a dry toothbrush
He grabbed the texture of a young hedgehog
He grabbed the slenderness of a silver needle.

To make his legs . . .
He grabbed the tickle of a bird's bony feather
He grabbed the dryness of a sandy desert
His legs were finished.

To grow his eyes . . .
He grabbed the miniature apple seed
He grabbed the darkness of a jet black night
He grabbed the readiness of a hunting cat.

For his walk . . .
He grabbed the silence of a still river
He grabbed the scuttling of a small rat
His walk was finished.

For the patterns on his back . . .
He grabbed the variety of a pack of Christmas cards
He grabbed the vibrant colours of a child's drawing
He grabbed the complexity of a stereo's speakers
    And spider was complete.

Susan Wright (9)
St Peter's CE (Aided) Primary School, Farnham

The Spooky Animal

The creatures crawl through the mist
Using their barbaric bodies
The glare of their spooky glowing eyes
Will frighten you out of your wits.

They will lie and wait for their prey,
Then they will pounce and dig their teeth
Into its flesh and blood
But they are not satisfied, they will hunt again.

The day comes again, they wait,
Till night they creep around in darkness,
The cubs are hungry the mother hunts more
For her cubs are ravenous.

Mason Redman (8)
St Peter's CE (Aided) Primary School, Farnham

Nature

I sometimes stop and wonder why
Little birds fly in the sky,
Why does the sun shine so bright?
Why do the stars come out at night?
How do little flowers know when to grow?

How or why I do not know,
Why does the tide go in and out?
What is nature all about?

Hayley Lynch (10)
St Polycarp's RC Primary School, Farnham

SEASONS

In spring it's time for blossom to grow,
It's time for the grass to grow once more,
Smell of snowdrops and sight of sunlight,
As I jump out of my front door.

In summer me and my friends go to play,
In gardens and in forests and in fields of green,
We laugh, we joke, we play and we run about,
And talk about what we've seen.

Autumn days, when the leaves are golden brown,
Fuschias are dying and roses too,
Jumping on piles of swept up leaves
And the things I love to do.

Winter is when the snow falls and water freezes,
People skating on the ponds and on a lake,
People singing Christmas carols at your front door,
Let's cut the Christmas cake.

Christopher Hopkin (10)
St Polycarp's RC Primary School, Farnham

ANIMALS

I love puppies and kitty cats,
But I don't like frogs or toads or rats.
I went out shopping with all my pets,
And while I was there, I walked to the vets.
He told me my animals were very nice
And he gave me a piece of useful advice.
'Look after your pets don't leave them alone,
And each day remember to give puppy a bone!'

Katie Allen (9)
St Polycarp's RC Primary School, Farnham

My Family

My dad
Never gets mad
My mum
Is never glum.

My grandma
Went to America
And my sister
Never missed her.

My brother
Likes Dad's mother
My grandad
Likes all rock bands.

My cat
Wears a funny hat
My dog
Plays with a hog.

Now I have told you
About my family
You can go now
And tell your family!

Sophie Crisp (10)
St Polycarp's RC Primary School, Farnham

METAL JUNK!

How old is that?
About forty years old I would say.
Door broken off,
Tyres blown down,
Front bonnet smashed up,
Crumpled side door,
Massive hole in roof,
Exhaust pipe on the floor,
Bent bumper,
Metal with lots of dents,
Windows smashed,
Paint scratched off,
I wonder what colour it was!

Will Park (9)
St Polycarp's RC Primary School, Farnham

DREADING . . .

Dreading that day,
On a Sunday night.
It seems so close,
That we dread it.
We wish it was Friday again,
But no.
It's still Sunday,
And that means . . .
School!

Rowena Leach (9)
St Polycarp's RC Primary School, Farnham

CRICKET

Cricket is my favourite sport,
It is a lot of fun,
Although when you're batting,
You can get very stunned.

My favourite part of cricket,
Is when I bowl,
Most people bowl fast,
While I bowl spin which is slow.

Fielding is just as fun,
You can get lots of catches,
Which as you probably know,
Can win lots of matches.

Wicket keeping is quite fun,
It might not be as good as bowling,
It might not be as good as batting
But still it is good enough for me.

Shaun Dole (9)
St Polycarp's RC Primary School, Farnham

FAIR

Why do grown-ups always say life's not fair when it is,
Every animal's got a talent
She's got hers and he's got his.
A monkey's got its tail,
The giraffe fights back with its neck,
And with its grace and magnificent speed
A dolphin can guard a ship's deck.

Alexandra Biffen (10)
St Polycarp's RC Primary School, Farnham

My Rabbits Mini And Milly

Mini and Milly
Sleep in a hutch
Sleep little bunnies
So soft to the touch.

Mini and Milly
Chomp on their bean
They look like a squirrel
When they have a little clean.

Mini and Milly
Have a little run,
Munching on the grass
In the boiling sun.

I bring them in
For a hug and a cud,
Then we cuddle up
Together like a rose in a bud.

Sleep now you've had a long day
Then in the morning
We can have a play.

Bethany Tod (10)
St Polycarp's RC Primary School, Farnham

WILD ANIMALS

Beware, the lion is watching
The tiger is cleaning its stripy fur,
The elephant is swishing its trunk
And you'll know when a snake is coming
Because the grass will stir.

Beware, the leopard is coming
The zebra is galloping nearby,
The dolphin is swimming in the sea
Watch out the fox is getting closer, quiet and sly.

Beware, the hyena is laughing
The parrot is flying past,
The camel is walking across the sandy desert
And the cheetah is running by, spotty and fast.

Be careful for the kangaroo is hopping by,
The koala is eating from the eucalyptus tree
And watch out for the sleeping crocodile
For if you wake him . . .

He might *snap!*

Lucy Warner (9)
St Polycarp's RC Primary School, Farnham

My Nintendo Gamecube

Every Saturday morning I wake up early,
To play on my Gamecube,
I run down the stairs and turn it on to play,
As I insert the disk into the Gamecube,
A *Tie* fighter blows up!

Bang!

I fly in my head as I fly an X-wing,
To the moon of Endor.

'Breakfast' calls Mum or Dad and suddenly,
The moon of Endor is far away,
I'm sitting on an ordinary chair,
In an ordinary room,
In an ordinary house,
I love my Nintendo Gamecube.

Richard Fisher (9)
St Polycarp's RC Primary School, Farnham

Sleepovers

We stay up all night laughing,
Pillowfights and makeovers are part of the fun.
Then we listen to secrets which make us giggle,
And then ghost stories which make us scared.

It's midnight let's have a feast,
Getting our crisps crushed in the sheets.
'Sssh!' cries Mum, 'it's getting late,'
Why does no one sleep at sleepovers?
Why don't you tell me?

Karen Lally (10)
St Polycarp's RC Primary School, Farnham

Clouds

When you and I were young
We thought the clouds were cotton wool
Stuck up in the sky,
Fluffy, white and always full.
But then one day we realised
That clouds were really vapour.
The water from the puddles,
The sun its evaporator.
When the clouds are really full,
It rains or pours,
And if it gets too cold,
It snows of course.
Clouds come in different shapes and sizes,
Some small, some tall, some thin,
Floating across the sky,
Flying, no engine, no wing.

Daniel Matthews (9)
St Polycarp's RC Primary School, Farnham

My Cat

My cat is very peculiar
He can even come to school with me
My cat can fit in my drawer
And actually go in my pocket
My cat can become as big as a giant
And become as tiny as a mouse
That's why my cat's peculiar.

Louisa Mayne (9)
St Polycarp's RC Primary School, Farnham

THE GREAT NETBALL MATCH

Nibbling your nails
Don't know what to do,
Ten minutes have passed
And they have scored two.
The ball is coming this way,
You're ready to catch,
Your friend throws it to you,
And guess what, you catch.
Your heart is beating fast,
You throw the ball up,
It spins round the net
And your friends jump up.
Our team was very happy
They cheered like a crowd.
And that was when
I felt funny inside.
A power of light shone
Into my eyes, I played
Like a star.
We won 12-5.

Anya Shahnazari (9)
St Polycarp's RC Primary School, Farnham

MY DAY AT SCHOOL

Every day we go to school,
Work, rest and play - it's really cool!
We have our lunch we read and write,
We try and try with all our might!
The school bell rings. We say
'Goodnight'
We really think that school's all right!

Lauren Weeks (8)
St Polycarp's RC Primary School, Farnham

On My Way To School One Day

On my way to school one day I saw a hairy caterpillar,
Suddenly I thought to myself
What would it feel like to be a hairy caterpillar?
Would I munch and crunch through leaves or crawl up and down trees
or hide away from birds or just sit and relax in the sun?

On my way to school one day I saw a big brown dog,
Suddenly I thought to myself
What would it feel like to be a big brown dog?
Would I run about or play and bark or go for walks or just sleep
in the house?

On my way to school one day I saw a black alley cat,
Suddenly I thought to myself
What it would feel like to be a black alley cat?
Would I jump on roofs or knock over bins or fight foxes or just
stroll about?

On my way to school one day I saw a bird with a red chest,
Suddenly I thought to myself
What would it feel like to be a bird with a red chest?
Would I fly high in the sky or grab worms from their hole or
sit in my nest or just sit on a tree?

On my way to school one day I saw a hairy, big, brown alley
caterpillardogcatbird with a red chest.

Tom Dawes (9)
St Polycarp's RC Primary School, Farnham

FIREWORKS

Fireworks swirling
Curving, curling,
I just watched eating a bun,
So Mum said I could choose one.
I don't know how to handle,
A fiery Roman Candle.
Catherine wheels go round and round,
But they don't make much sound.
Rockets go up to the stars,
They might be able to reach Mars.
Bangers make such a noise,
They're used to scare some kids by boys.
I chose a sparkler just for me
They're not dangerous but great to see.

Sarah Hay (9)
St Polycarp's RC Primary School, Farnham

TV PROGRAMMES

Some TV programmes are brill like The Simpsons & Tucker.

Some TV programmes are boring like the news and documentaries.

Some TV programmes are funny like Only Fools and Horses & Fawlty Towers.

Some TV programmes are sad like Children's Hospital & soppy films.

But some TV programmes are all of these rolled into one.

Edward Clark (9)
St Polycarp's RC Primary School, Farnham

The Cat And The Rat

It was a cold winter's night,
And the moon was bright,
When I saw the cat,
Chasing a rat.
The rat then said 'This is no fun,
I'll chase you and make you run.'
The cat said to the rat,
'If you can do that, I'll eat my hat.
So give it a go.
I bet you will say, 'No.'
The rat then said 'I will give it a try,
But I don't know why,
Are you having a laugh?
Do you think I'm daft?'
And he opened his jaw
And bit the cat's paw.

Max Cooper (10)
St Polycarp's RC Primary School, Farnham

Where Is The Bogeyman?

Where is the bogeyman?
Is he in my bed? No.
Would he be in my wardrobe? No.
Is he in the bathroom, or maybe down the loo? No.
Mum said, 'Dinner's ready, come and get it.'
Could he be in my dinner? No.
'Mum have you seen the bogeyman?' No.
A friend comes over, 'Would you know where the
Bogeyman could be?' No.
Oh I forgot where I left him, he is in the picky place, the germ place . . .
my nose!

Mathew Hand (9)
St Polycarp's RC Primary School, Farnham

THE PERFECT LIFE FOR ME

My name is Rose and I'm not very old,
But I've moved house once,
My bed is so comfortable
And I get all the water I need.

Summer is my favourite season,
I always relax in the sun,
I also like spring
Because I meet new friends.

I hate autumn and winter,
Because something bad usually happens,
Like nearly freezing in the snow
And almost dying because
I have to have a haircut.

You thought I was a human!

Well you're wrong,
I'm a flower all right,
And my bed's in soil
I live outside and I'm free!

I get watered each day,
And you'll understand about the seasons
I moved house from a pot,
To the open outside,
With my friends beside me,
All the time.
I'm free in the garden
Yes I'm free!

Suzanne Burroughs (10)
St Polycarp's RC Primary School, Farnham

Seaside Poem

The sky is blue,
Brightly the sun is shining,
My friends are here too.

The crabs scuttle on the sand,
In the sea,
And on your hand.

The waves calm as they approach the shore,
They crash against the rocks,
I don't like them any more.

The fishes swim smoothly in the sea,
Fast and slow,
Lively as can be.

The golden sand lies peacefully,
Until a creature comes,
Shuffling on it carelessly.

Making sandcastles with your pail,
Digging the sand with your spade,
Or making a great big whale.

Rocks are sharp and wet,
You can slip easily,
I can bet.

The seaweed is slimy and green,
It gets washed up by the sea,
Sometimes the feel makes you scream.

As the sun sets,
And the moon comes up,
I finish the day all tucked up.

Rachel Cauldwell (9)
St Polycarp's RC Primary School, Farnham

Holiday Mayhem

When you're going on holiday it can be such a hassle,
For you have to park your car,
Wrestle luggage, queue forever,
Scream at kids and hang around.

Show your passport, what a terrible photo,
Then all the bags are X-rayed,
Metal detector goes *beep,*
Hooray look there's McDonald's, please, please, please!

Yippee a gate for the plane,
Quick let's get on the flight,
Gate 25, that's where we need to go,
Where's my boarding pass?

Let's get our seats, hey that's my seat,
Our seat belts go *click,*
Sit back comfortably, here we go,
On the runway now.

We are going faster and faster and up in the air,
Wow we are actually flying,
Yummy snacks are coming down the aisle,
Thank you for the grub.

It's very loud in here, be quiet,
Good now I can read a book and have a nap,
Zzzzzzzzzz, yawn, we are in France,
Hooray, let's go and get our bags, goodbye!

Luca Scardarella (9)
St Polycarp's RC Primary School, Farnham

Me

I'm told I am vivacious,
I am usually intelligent,
My mum says I have self respect,
I always make my friends laugh,
They say I'm hilarious,
I'm told I was astonishing in my play,
I hope I become a lady-like person,
I have a wild imagination,
All my teachers say I'm talented,
I am always affectionate to my mother,
I like working independently,
I'm a loyal person to my family and friends,
Usually I'm obedient,
I'm always respectful to other adults.

Vishali Tailor (9)
St Polycarp's RC Primary School, Farnham

A Winter's Day

A gloomy winter's day
So cold and grey
Frosty cars that look so white
Shimmering in the sunlight
Snow covering the ground
Just right for running around
Children playing in the snow
Until it is time to go
Leaving their snowmen
Hoping they will see them again
Now it is time for bed
Maybe more snow ahead.

Adenais Vachon (9)
St Polycarp's RC Primary School, Farnham

School Rules

All the teachers are better than the rest,
You're not allowed to cheat in a maths test.
No coloured socks or laces, no trainers, no jeans
No smiling faces.

No singing, no make-up, no jewellery, no bell ringing
No music, no chewing, no spitting, no telly,
No making rude noises especially if they're smelly.

No chatting back to the teacher
As they think you are a creature.

All spellings correct and neatly too,
From the back of my hand
To the front of my shoe
All lunch boxes on the rack,
And rucksacks on your back.

All homework in the morning tray,
Think to yourself it's a lovely day
No throwing snowballs at each other
Only at your sister or your brother.

It's the end of the day and it's time to meet Mum
We get our coats and I'm not feeling very glum
I hope there are lots of sweets in the car
Thank goodness our house is not too far.

Rosie Whittle (8)
St Polycarp's RC Primary School, Farnham

HANNAH

Sometimes I feel happy and popular
And sometimes I feel sad and lame
My uncle says I do show off
My auntie says I've got a cough
My brother says I go boo hoo
My sister says that's for you
My mum and dad always say I eat too much
But when they do I just blush!
My grandma always spends too much
She never stops to say that's enough,
Now dear till another day
What grandad teaches me is *brill*
He gives me lots of hugs when I'm ill
I have two great friends one of them is Rosie
When she comes round she is totally wow!
Sophie is a really good mate
When I put my earrings on she says
'The dolphin ones are great!'

Hannah Trafford (8)
St Polycarp's RC Primary School, Farnham

MY SISTER IS MY OWNER IS MY SISTER

My sister is my owner
She tells me what to do
I've been her doll,
I've been her pet,
I've been her pupil too.
I really do not like it
I have told her lots and lots
She treats me like a baby
Even though I'm not.

Emma Brew (9)
St Polycarp's RC Primary School, Farnham

THE WIZARD'S SWEET SHOP

Inside the wizard's sweet shop
Through that open door
Sweets your heart desires
Lying on the floor.

Blue cherries, bubblegum
(refuses to burst for weeks)
Liquorice wands
Honey flavoured (*mmm* very sweet).

Twinkle, twinkle
Little star,
Sherbet shooting stars
Right you are.

The sherbet shooting stars
Are truly amazing,
Coming in all sorts of flavourings
Mushroom soup
Bat's blood
Brussel sprouts (yuck)
And much much more.

Now that you know about this magical sweet shop
Have a look around
There's many more sweets to amaze you,
So see what can be found!

Felicity M Pollock (9)
St Polycarp's RC Primary School, Farnham

SUMMER IN THE SANDS!

I once spent a summer in the sands,
Watching people getting good tans.

Lazing in the calm warm waves,
Trying to catch some crabs in cool dark caves.

Licking ice cream till they were all gone
Getting very hot while the sun shone on.

Building sandcastles till the end of the day
Persuading my brother to make them my way.

Jumping for the ball which was just out of reach,
Resting on a lilo lying on the beach.

Sailing along in bright blue boats,
Lots of children needing swimming floats.

At last I had to say goodbye,
But I swam a race and it was a tie.

I once spent a summer in the sands,
Dreaming of people in far off lands.

Stephanie Stone (8)
St Polycarp's RC Primary School, Farnham

THE MAKEOVER

'Hello Sue!
Want to come round?
I'm having a makeover
How does that sound?

I will do your hair
In purple streaks,
You will be able to keep it in
For weeks and weeks.

If you really want
I will pierce your ears,
I'm a professional
So don't burst into tears!

You can have a facial
With cucumber on your eyes,
And listen to music,
I am not telling lies!'

'Of course Amy
I'd love to come,
I would really like a makeover
I will ask my mum.'

Emma White (8)
St Polycarp's RC Primary School, Farnham

Spring Is In The Air

Spring is in the air
The birds are everywhere
Sitting in the trees
Watching all the bees
Looking for a nest
With Mr Robin Redbreast.

Spring is in the air
The birds are everywhere.
The blackbird sings his song,
All the day long.
He saves his energy at night
To give us much delight.
All day long
He will sing his song.

Emily Richardson (9)
St Polycarp's RC Primary School, Farnham

Autumn Leaves

Autumn leaves are falling
Red, brown and yellow
The trees are almost bare
It looks so dull out there.

Autumn leaves are falling
They are all down now,
How I look forward to
Seeing trees green once more.

Sabrina Mitchell (9)
St Polycarp's RC Primary School, Farnham

BATTLEGROUND 1815

Slowly Napoleon's brave, tired army advances,
Through black smoke and thick mud, on they go.
The cavalry charges and the enemy meets them with their lances,
Bang, bang, booms the cannon, on and on they go.

Wellington watches, plans and gives his orders,
Waiting for the French, to meet their foe.
'We'll stop them lads from getting to our borders!'
Bang, bang, booms the cannon, on and on they go.

The general rides out upon his proud stallion,
Men fall shouting swear words, crawling low,
British lined up regiments and a battalion,
Bang, bang, booms the cannon, on and on they go.

Mighty Blücher comes to save the day,
His black flags charging from the wood,
Cannons fire, down the French bodies lay
Bang, bang, boomed the cannon, red flowed the blood.

Christopher Evans (8)
St Polycarp's RC Primary School, Farnham

FOOTBALL

F ootball is fun for all
O ver the post goes the ball
O ff the goalie's whopping kick
T he football volleys with a flick
B ut although the skill is fair
A nd the ball flies through the air it
L obs and skims the goalie's ear then
L ots of fans scream, shout and cheer.

Simon Daruvala (9)
St Polycarp's RC Primary School, Farnham

I Wonder

I wonder where I am?
I wander, I wonder, I wander
For there is nothing else to wonder
For dogs are hanging upside down!
I wander, I wonder, I wander
And rabbits are going round and round!
I wander, I wonder, I wander.

The trees are purple, the ground is blue.
My brain is pumping for I wonder too.
For I do not know what I should do
And all the cats are saying, 'Boo!'
I think I am in, now let me look
Because I have read it in a book
I wonder, I wander, I wonder.

May Clyne (8)
St Polycarp's RC Primary School, Farnham

A Winning Goal

All I can hear
Is 'Down the line!'
and 'Take it all the way!'
I sprint like lightning
All I can see is the
gruesome goalkeeper guarding
his neglected net.
My right foot boots the ball
into the corner of the empty net.
Now all I can hear is,
'Yeeeeh Freddie!'

Freddie Marshall (9)
St Polycarp's RC Primary School, Farnham

COMPUTERS

I can play Robot Wars
and Star Wars Galactic Battles.
I can play Lego Racers
I can play anything.

I like to type lots of things,
I think it's lots of fun.
I can type made-up stories
I can type anything.

I always use the Internet,
when I need to find an answer.
I go on the Internet for fun,
I can Internet anything.

If I didn't have a computer,
I would go completely mad.
If I had to live without one,
I would be really, really sad.

Jonathan Birt (9)
St Polycarp's RC Primary School, Farnham

THE FISH AND ME

A fish said 'You're freaky!'
as I swam in the sea.
He surprised me with his croaky voice,
so I banged him on the knee.

He screamed at me and said 'Get off!'
I said, 'Be quiet!' to him.
Little boys should not hit out
and fishes should not talk but swim.

James Frisby (9)
St Polycarp's RC Primary School, Farnham

The Sun And The Moon

The sun shines bright
But goes down at night.
The moon takes its place
With a silvery face.
The sun comes back and lights up the world
Then the moon comes out with a smile that's curled.

I wake up with the sun out again.
I switch my alarm clock off
Then twiddle my pen.
I go and do my hands and face
Then go down looking a *disgrace.*
Then I have my day at school.
After I play in the swimming pool.
Then I go home and go to sleep
Cuddle my ted
Then the moon puts me to bed.

George Hopper (9)
St Polycarp's RC Primary School, Farnham

Cats And Dogs

Dogs and cats are different in many ways,
Some have owners, some are strays.
They come in different colours.
Some have stripes and spots.
But all the Dalmatians just have plain dots!
I have a cat, it's just black and white, with long silky hair,
But my sister says it's as fluffy as a bear!
I wish I had another cat, one with stripes and spots,
So it would look like a jaguar and other times it would not!

Lily Livingston (8)
St Polycarp's RC Primary School, Farnham

Jumping Rabbits

Mini and Milly,
All fat and clean,
Their favourite food,
Is a jumping bean.

Such a bright day,
Frolicking around,
Leaping and jumping,
It's a merry-go-round.

The flowers are out,
The sun still shone,
Play and play,
Time's almost gone!

Sleep precious bunnies,
It's been a long day,
Wait for another one
Then we will play!

Sophie Tod (8)
St Polycarp's RC Primary School, Farnham

All About Football

F ootball is one of the best sports
O wen is a good football player
O wen is number 10 in football
T ottenham's team is good
B eckham is a brill player
A ll the teams rule
L ots of footballers are very good
L iverpool are cool.

Elliott Jones (9)
St Polycarp's RC Primary School, Farnham

THE CROCODILE

The crocodile goes like this and that
He never says 'Sorry'
He always says, 'Take that.'

He eats and eats and never stops
He likes to take you by surprise
And will make you jump and hop.

When he begins to eat
Crunchity, crunch, munchity munch
Off will go your feet.

Next he eats your tummy,
Full of all your dinner.
'Yum, yum, that was very yummy.'

Last of all he eats your head.
Finishes you off.
Now you are dead!

Francesca Pipkin (8)
St Polycarp's RC Primary School, Farnham

AUTUMN SEA

The sea has silky seaweed sparkly and blue
Sea eyes are exactly like you
Jumping dolphins jump from above the saltings
Down down in the deep sea submarines are
making their way through
Octopuses tangling up with their tickly legs
and arms.

Kieran Pickford (9)
St Polycarp's RC Primary School, Farnham

Children At The Beach

Children play upon the beach
The soft sand at their feet.
The sun glitters over the waves
As they crash upon their feet.

Children look upon the sands
To see the seashell large and small
As the waves repeat and fall
Children running up and down
To catch a crab to bite their toe.

The day gets dark they all run home
To see their mummy and daddy again . . .

Francesca Brain (9)
St Polycarp's RC Primary School, Farnham

Autumn Leaves

Leaves hanging off the trees.
Squirrels gathering their nuts.
Badgers burying food for hibernation.
Foxes in their dens.
Birds flying west for winter.
Soon it will be the harvest.
Everyone collecting their fruit and veg.
There are loads of colours around.
Leaves are everywhere, it's beautiful.
I run and run around.
I throw the leaves.

Esme Dunne (9)
St Polycarp's RC Primary School, Farnham

Snow

Snow is great
To appreciate
One, two, three, four five,
But what would happen when you're alive?
Snow is great
To appreciate.

Six, seven, eight, nine, ten
One time it will melt again.
Snow is great
To appreciate.

Ten, nine, eight, seven six
But everyone is in a mix
Snow is great
To appreciate.

Five, four, three, two, one
Snow is great fun!

Emily Morris (8)
St Polycarp's RC Primary School, Farnham

Fat Cat

I've got a fat cat
That can't get through the door,
Maybe it's because all she does is snore.
I've got a fat cat that lives next door
He drives a Mercedes that starts with a roar.

Helena Pickford (9)
St Polycarp's RC Primary School, Farnham

AUTUMN LEAVES

Autumn leaves dry and crumbly falling off the trees
twirling on the ground like a little tornado,
the wind slowly picks up some leaves and they fly,
then the wind gently stops,
and the leaves fall and land softly on the ground.

Corinne Nelson (8)
St Polycarp's RC Primary School, Farnham

ICE CREAM

Is it pink, is it blue, is it green like shampoo?
If it's tasty, eat it hasty! If it's hot, let it rot!
If it's cold *put it in a bowl!* Is it creamy
Soft and dreamy? If it's light *take a bite!*
What is it? *Ice cream!*

Sam Hearn (8)
St Polycarp's RC Primary School, Farnham

THE SKY

The sky is blue with white puffy clouds.
The clouds move slowly like a long glacier.
With frosty white peaks.
The sun shines like a meteorite closing in.
The night-time sky is full of stars like ten thousand fragments
of diamonds.

Dominic Guttridge (8)
St Polycarp's RC Primary School, Farnham

The Big Fight

When the sky strikes black
and we begin to be flat
All the ghosts come out
we have a great big fight
It is surely bright
but they fight like a knight
We begin to win
and they stand on a pin
They begin to win the tin
the pin starts to win
The fin starts to sing
like a bird on the wing with a ping.

Laurence Hills (8)
St Polycarp's RC Primary School, Farnham

Football

There is a game I love to play
In fact I play it every day
I am much better now that
I have learnt to pass
Playing on fantastic grass
I am quite good at it now
That I am very fit
It is football don't you see
That is so important to me.

Laura Heron (9)
St Polycarp's RC Primary School, Farnham

SWEETS

Sweets are yummy scrummy
and lovely in my tummy.
They come in lots of shapes and sizes
and sometimes in birthday surprises.

Some are big and some are small
sometimes chewy and very gooey.
But when you go down to the corner shop
there's just too much to choose,
but the ones I like the best are the one penny chews.

When I go to pay,
the one thing I must not forget
is to get my family something
or I will surely regret.

Eloise Rudd (9)
St Polycarp's RC Primary School, Farnham

ONE, TWO

One, two
Lost my shoe
Three, four
Going to the shore
Five, six
I eat a Twix
Seven, eight
Going to be late
Nine, ten
I met Sven.

Conor Phillips (10)
St Polycarp's RC Primary School, Farnham

GHOSTS!

Most people will tell you that
Ghosts are not real - they say this because
they have never seen one, those who may have
seen one are frightened so they yell
Ghosts!
Some people believe ghosts only
live in old scary houses,
others believe ghosts may be anywhere -
still others believe ghosts are only *myths*

Two boys and a girl saw this old house
they did not want to go up to the front door
because they were frightened
the girl called them 'chicken',
to prove they were not chicken
they all went up to the front door
the door made a creaking sound when it opened
in the hallway they awakened the *ghost*
of Screaming Lord Sutch!

Adam Miller (10)
St Polycarp's RC Primary School, Farnham

MEGGIE'S FRUITS

A pples are fun with a bun
P ears are fun when they're juicy
P eas are round and green like your bogeys
L egs are used to run and walk, they're not used to kick and talk
E ggy Meggie is very stressy, what can we do to help
S he is stressy like a dessy so she turns to dust.

Jack McClure (8)
St Polycarp's RC Primary School, Farnham

GOLDEN LIGHT

Golden light,
streaming through the trees,
gladdening the world
and the fishes in the seas.

Shining from the sun,
over leaves and grass
and sharing all its loveliness
with others who may pass.

Generous and caring,
helping all the poor,
who feel sad and lonely
to feel happiness once more.

Glinting off the raindrops,
the oceans and the dew
and helping Earth's inhabitants
to once again feel new.

Martha Hearn (11)
St Polycarp's RC Primary School, Farnham

LOOKING FOR A FRIEND

I lost a friend
Now I am looking; looking for a new friend.
I need a friend.

Seeking someone, to be my friend.
I need a friend. I need a friend because
I need help with my poem.

Edwin Jones (10)
St Polycarp's RC Primary School, Farnham

The Four Seasons

Tiny lambs sprinting free,
Baby rabbits in the field,
I hope you won't meet a bee
And the farmer gets a good yield.

Sunshine beaming down,
Clouds fluffy too,
Muddy river all brown,
Children playing at the zoo.

Leaves are falling very quick,
Animals in hibernation,
Cats giving themselves a lick,
People going on winter vacation.

Snow is falling very deep,
Flakes landing on the ground,
You won't be seeing many sheep,
Unless you look around.

Nicole Sarsons (10)
St Polycarp's RC Primary School, Farnham

Homework

H elp, I've got to do my homework:
O h no! I really can't do it:
M um can you help me?
E easy peasy, you can do that!
W ork, work, work what more can she give us?
O ut to play soon, I've nearly finished.
R ead it through, check spellings and punctuation:
K eep smiling I've finished.

Stephanie Jane Harrison (9)
St Polycarp's RC Primary School, Farnham

A Walk In The Park

A walk in the park with my family and dog,
Gives me the spring feeling, moving away from the winter fog.
The sheep and the cows eating all day,
With the horses as well, munching on hay,
The smell of cows is really quite strong!
I wish I hadn't come along,
Oranges and reds find a way to
Scatter across the 5 o'clock sky,
A sunset so beautiful we have to stand and stare,
And then the sky is bare.
The sun completely disappearing
And all becomes dark.

Rachel Myers (10)
St Polycarp's RC Primary School, Farnham

Mysterious Clouds

Looking up I see the face looking down at me.
Big round eyes, a short stubby nose and
A mouth that smiles at me.

I look again, I see a dog
With a little tail and great big ears.

I look again, this time I see
A tree with long branches and crystal leaves.

But when I look again there is
Nothing there but blue sky and sunshine,
All my clouds have disappeared.

Matthew Barton (9)
St Polycarp's RC Primary School, Farnham

WHERE SHALL WE GO ON HOLIDAY?

Where shall we go on holiday?
We haven't booked one yet
Where shall we go on holiday?
I am really starting to fret.

We should go to Spain or Las Vegas,
Or possibly even LA,
Australia, Rwanda,
Or maybe we can go somewhere
Where we can get good lasagne.

Where shall we go on holiday?
We haven't booked one yet
Where shall we go on holiday?
I am really starting to fret.

We could go to Italy,
Or perhaps go to France,
Belgium, Wales
Or go to see an amphibian
With real big scales.

I know, let's stay at home this time.
We could see all the sights
The castle, the wood,
The lakes and the market
Wouldn't that be good?

I know where to go on holiday
We don't need to book one at all
I know where to go on holiday
I really don't need to bawl.

Alexandra McCourt (11)
St Polycarp's RC Primary School, Farnham

Horror Books

Horror books are just blood and gore
But when you read on your body
Screams for more
They're full of ghosts and ghouls
And sometimes red eyed wolves.

Horror books are full of blood and guts
They'll scare the pants off you
They're full of mindless zombies
And sometimes bogie monsters.

Horror books are scary things
They're not about fairies with pretty pink wings
They'll give you nightmares
And never lovely dreams.

Andrew Sisley (11)
St Polycarp's RC Primary School, Farnham

Rabbits

A wonderful way to spend a day,
Lovely and sunny in the month of May,
Hopping around the trees as they sway,
Looking for friends that are out to play.

Sniffing a flower here and there,
Twitching their noses in the fresh air,
Their bodies stop as they stare,
Over the hills that are ever so bare.

Rebecca Ledgerwood (11)
St Polycarp's RC Primary School, Farnham

SCARE!

The moon shines bright,
In the middle of the night,
The ghosts come out to play,
The werewolves howl,
Ghouls are on the prowl,
Witches are here to stay.

Devils chant,
Wizards grant,
1000 evil spells,
Black cats miaow,
Goblins pinch me . . . *ow!*
The witch's potion really smells.

Cobwebs surround,
Genies all around,
Skeletons rattle themselves,
Pumpkins alight,
There's monsters' delight,
With an army of little elves.

Vampires everywhere,
Frankenstein's over there,
Spiders creep up the stair,
Dragons roar,
There's dust galore,
Watch out! *Don't get a scare!*

Amy-Clair Jones (10)
St Polycarp's RC Primary School, Farnham

TISHA

I have a cat called Tisha
She came from the RSPCA
She's as black as the night
But troublesome is her middle name
Oh Tisha!

She climbed up the Christmas tree
And opened half the presents
Raced up my brother's brand new curtains
Then abseiled down my mum's best belt
Oh Tisha!

The worst thing of all
Was when Nan came to stay,
Tisha found her false teeth
And then ran away
Oh Tisha!

Hannah Quarterman (10)
St Polycarp's RC Primary School, Farnham

THE BEAR

Cuddly fur, doesn't purr
Wet nose, big toes.
Small eyes, fat thighs,
Known as grizzly,
Coat's frizzy.
What am I?

Millie Merceron (10)
St Polycarp's RC Primary School, Farnham

By The Sea

My holiday house is such a place to be,
It's miles and miles away,
But it's worth it in West Wales by the sea.
We walk by the beach happily,
Just my dad and me.

It's fun to be by the sandy seaside
And to watch the seagulls gracefully glide.
We see the sailing boats gently sailing by,
Their tall masts scratching the sky.

I like to play in the sparkling rock pools
And watch the hermit crabs fighting duels.
Children playing on the sand,
Building castles very grand!

How I love being by the sea,
My sisters, mother, dad and me.
The beach is my favourite place to be,
How I long to be in my holiday house,
By the sea.

Thomas Torjüssen (8)
St Polycarp's RC Primary School, Farnham

Ice

Ice blows its icy freezing breath on everything,
He makes it very cold for everyone,
Sometimes Ice has a party with snow and frightens
Everybody when they are trying to get to sleep,
In the morning he is too tired to blow ice onto everything,
So Ice just breaths his cold breath
And then goes back to sleep.

Christine Nelson (11)
St Polycarp's RC Primary School, Farnham

SING

When dawn approaches
They sing their hearts out
When dusk approaches
They sing their hearts out

When the sun is high
They sing their hearts out
When the sun is low
They sing their hearts out

Blue tit or peacock
They sing their hearts out
Robin or parrot
They sing their hearts out

Young or old
They sing their hearts out
Boy or girl
They sing their hearts out

Colourful or dull
They sing their hearts out
Beautiful or ugly
They sing their hearts out

If they are a bird
They will sing their hearts out
For all birds
Sing their hearts out.

James Kirrane (11)
St Polycarp's RC Primary School, Farnham

Winter

Listen!
Can you hear the whistling wind
Whirling at the window
Look!
Can you see the looping leaves
Leaping over the lawn
Feel!
Can you feel the shivering
Snow sneaking up your spine
Taste!
Can you taste the spicy soup
Swimming into your stomach.

Elizabeth G Farrant (7)
St Polycarp's RC Primary School, Farnham

Storm

He comes with wind and rain.
Thunder tags along too.

Thunder charges along the street
Like a heard of angry bulls.

Rain comes next
Drenching everything in its path
And making people's vision blurred.

Wind comes last, howling like a wolf
And blowing rain around.

Alexander Haddon (11)
St Polycarp's RC Primary School, Farnham

The Witch

She comes by night,
In fearsome fight,
In garments black as pitch.

The queen of doom,
Upon her broom,
A wild and wicked witch.

Her pointy nose,
Her spiky toes,
Her skin as hard as rock.

Her lips are red,
It seems she's dead
Until you hear her knock.

She cast a spell,
Or so they tell,
Upon that house that night.

The queen of doom,
Upon her broom,
A wild and wicked sight!

Elése Price (10)
St Polycarp's RC Primary School, Farnham

ARCHIE

We're going to get a puppy
And Archie is his name,
He likes the rain and sunshine,
I hope he's very tame,
The first day we saw him,
He slept all the time,
When we take him from his mum,
I hope he doesn't whine.

I love him very much,
I wish he'll never die.
He likes to chew my fingers,
But only for a while.

My mum wants to take him for walks.
My dad wants to have him in his study
And my sister wants to have lots of talks.
I hope he's very happy
Because he's only a puppy.

I love him very much,
I hope he'll never die,
He likes to chew my fingers,
But only for a while.

Katie Heron (11)
St Polycarp's RC Primary School, Farnham

CHOCOLATE

Chocolate, chocolate
You're wonderful stuff
I love you, chocolate
I can't get enough
You're covered with love
Chocolate, chocolate
Oh give me some more.

Chocolate, chocolate
Piled high up on my hand
You're melting as fast as you can
I can't stop eating you
Chocolate, chocolate
I think you are great.

Chocolate, chocolate
I love you
You're slishy and sloshy
Delicious and great
I gobble you down
Oh, I can't get enough
Chocolate, chocolate
You're wonderful stuff.

Claire Arnold (10)
St Polycarp's RC Primary School, Farnham

THE BEAUTIFUL DAY

The shimmering sun that shines down
Is making all the children frown
Lilies trickling like never before
Sun burning, making skin sore
Whilst the sun is powerful and gleaming
The children can be seen playfully screaming.

Adults resting in a peaceful way
Watching the world turn, day-by-day
As day turns to night, the moon starts glowing
With the sound of the river, gently flowing
Birds are starting to go to sleep
High in the trees, without a peep.

Spiky hedgehogs curled up on the ground
Making not a single sound
People are packing up, ready to go
But children are shouting, *'No! No! No!'*
Mums saying, 'We'd better move fast,'
It's time to go to bed at last.

Chantelle de-Filippis (8)
St Polycarp's RC Primary School, Farnham

MILLY MONKEY'S WORLD

There was a monkey called Milly
And she was a silly Billy
She sat all alone
But her mum said, 'Come home!'
At night she couldn't sleep
She played a game called Peep
And went to sleep with Billy the funny sheep
As she dreamed she was Little Bo Peep.

Charlotte Mary Goode (8)
St Polycarp's RC Primary School, Farnham

THE ROOK

Something magical about it
Tiles blue on towers tall
Door big enough for a giant
Dungeons wide and cavernous hall

Studs and belts were polished silver
Blue peeking out from behind the cloud
Green wavy sea, light and frothy
Dragon in a window proud

Woods surrounded all around
Up against the walls of stone
Vines curling round the pillars
Gold upon the king's throne

A thousand steps laid bottom to top
A castle with a turret
Looking close it seemed to sparkle
Something magical about it.

Bret Cameron (8)
St Polycarp's RC Primary School, Farnham

FOOTBALL

Football is a good sport,
It is very well taught.
Footballers are in a team,
Some can be mean.
Footballers have lots of skills,
When they win a match there are lots of thrills.
When footballers play,
It could be a rainy day.

Kieran Press (7)
St Polycarp's RC Primary School, Farnham

FOOTBALL CRAZY

My brother's football crazy
He plays for Rushmoor Saints
He plays football everywhere
It drives my dad insane.

I'm football crazy
I also play for Rushmoor Saints
I play football all day long
It drives my mum mad.

The garden is the football pitch
The lounge and hall as well
There are two broken outside lights
One smashed window too.

Louis Quarterman (8)
St Polycarp's RC Primary School, Farnham

WINTER FUN

When you go skiing you will see
All different people waiting to ski
I was one of these people once
And I might be one again.

When you go skiing you will see
All different kinds of snow
Some will be soft, some will be hard
And some will be slushy too.

Oh I wish it would snow every day
And that would make me very happy.

Tim Sarnowski (7)
St Polycarp's RC Primary School, Farnham

My Little Sister

My little sister is very naughty
And she goes on the potty.

She loves flowers
And likes to climb towers.

My little sister has yellow hair,
It's as scruffy as a bear.

She wears holey tops
And trousers with spots.

She eats chips
And apple pips.

I only have one little sister,
But if she wasn't here, I'd miss her.

Clare Besley (7)
St Polycarp's RC Primary School, Farnham

Spooky

The moon is out
The sky is dark
The dogs bark
And owls hoot
Dead man's boots.

A scream in the night
When darkness falls
Funny goblins and
Witches' shawls.

Alexander Lewis (7)
St Polycarp's RC Primary School, Farnham

FOOD

My sister likes all her greens
But I only like French green beans!
My friend Sian can see in the dark,
She eats lots of carrots, even in the park!
My grandma with her silver-grey hair,
Peels the most delicious pear!
My wonderful daddy loves his beef steak,
But his scrambled egg is a crunchy mistake!
The fantastic thing about my poppa
Is whatever he cooks its always a whopper!
Chocolates and sweets are my treat,
So tell me now what you like to eat.

Olivia O'Carroll (8)
St Polycarp's RC Primary School, Farnham

MY MUM DOES EVERYTHING

My mum cleans and dusts the house
She takes me to school in a car, not cool
And when I get home I go in the pool.
When I'm going to school I wish we were going in a Laguna
So we would get there sooner.
My mum cooks the most delicious dinners
They surely are the winners.
She hangs the clothes on the washing line
I wish I was Tarzan, I'd use it for a vine.
My mum does all the work while I sit and watch the telly
And I hear a rumbling coming from my belly.
My mum is really quite brilliant because she does everything!

James Mather (8)
St Polycarp's RC Primary School, Farnham

AUTUMN IS OVER AND WINTER IS HERE

Autumn is now over.
The leaves on the trees have changed from green
to bright orange and dull brown.
They have all fallen to the ground
and been swept away by the wind.
Now all the trees are bare and cold
and swaying to and fro.

Winter is now here.
The weather is really cold and windy
we wrap ourselves up warm.
Everyone has bright red cheeks and pink noses
when they are out in the cold.
The best thing about winter is when
the bright, white snow falls from the sky.
You look out in the morning and see
your very own wonderland.

Amie Boyle (7)
St Polycarp's RC Primary School, Farnham

FOOTBALL

When you score a goal the crowd goes wild
And now it is getting very, very mild
As well it's getting very cloudy, *oh no!*
Everyone is crying, they are in the lead
And they are biting things like hands
Tea cakes and popcorn, lots of other foods,
Soccer stuff and drinks
And it is the best match.

Alexander Jaeggi (8)
St Polycarp's RC Primary School, Farnham

Flowers

I like the blue of the bluebells
in the sunny spring.
I feel happy looking at the flowers,
I could sit and look for hours and hours.
I like the daffodils they make me think
of the shiny, bright sun.
I like the red, red rose as I bend down
and smell with my nose.
I feel as if I am in fairy land.
I wish I had all these flowers but
it could not be.
I really want these flowers
all for me.

Isobel Dossett (7)
St Polycarp's RC Primary School, Farnham

The Nasty Pear

I had a nasty nightmare,
it was about a nasty pear.
When I bit it, my hair went square,
it gave my mum a nasty scare.
The pear set off a flare,
half way down the stair.
If my mum is very good,
I'll share my pear with her there,
half way down the stair.
PS
Beware: the nasty *pear!*

Thomas Hopkin (8)
St Polycarp's RC Primary School, Farnham

When I Grow Up

When I grow up I would like to be
a painter painting portraits
or a skater on ice skates.

When I grow up I would like to be
a zookeeper or a vet.
I like the idea of being a farmer
but outside I might get wet.

When I grow up I would like to be
an archaeologist digging in the sun,
that might be fun.
My friends say I am bossy
so I might want to be a teacher
but that takes a special kind of creature.

When I grow up I would like to be
a gymnast winning medals
feeling very, very proud.
Around the arena there will be a very big crowd.

Right now I don't know what to be
but it's really, really up to me.

Clare Kavanagh (8)
St Polycarp's RC Primary School, Farnham

Galloping Free

Galloping free with the breeze in my mane
Faster and faster the wind calls my name.
'Spirit, Spirit come out to play
The sun's coming up so let's welcome the day.'

Rearing and bucking with my legs in the air.
The eagle, my friend swooped down from his lair
He dived and he shrieked, 'Come race with me,
Just for the fun of being free!'

We rushed and weaved, twisted and turned
Joy in my heart with fire burned
And when evening comes and playtime's gone
We'll dream of the warmth of tomorrow's dawn.

Rosie Stammers (8)
St Polycarp's RC Primary School, Farnham

Fright

It's a quiet sound on the ground,
It's a scary sound in the town,
That's the time when you've found,
That's the time when you frown!

It's a dark sight in the night,
It's a bright sight of the light,
That's the time when you feel tight,
That's the time when you might get a fright!

Liam Wong (8)
St Polycarp's RC Primary School, Farnham

FARM POEM

Once there was a farm, on the farm there was a pig,
The pig was big and fat.
There also was a horse who always wore a wig
When it was sunny he took off his wig and put on a hat.

The lambs are warm and woolly,
They're small and very fast.
One of the cows chases the lambs
And so he's called the big bully.
When he's chasing them, if they stop,
He will be running so fast that he'll run right past.

When the dogs are helping with the sheep they are very loud,
The lambs are frightened and not at all bold.
When the sheep are all cooped up the dogs look very proud.
If a lamb gets lost, the dog will find it and take it back to the farmer.
The sheep is so scared it listens to what it's told.

Laura Flynn (8)
St Polycarp's RC Primary School, Farnham

THE WINTER'S NIGHT

As the moon comes out and the light comes down
the twinkling stars are all about

As the snow comes shivering down, down, down
children look out and are in a trance as the snow hits the ground

As the flaky flakes float down to the lakes and land below
the glittery flakes shiver down as they hit the earth and turn into snow

This is a winter's night.

Lydia Thomas (7)
St Polycarp's RC Primary School, Farnham

Sheba

I call my friend the smiley man,
He is seventy-two,
He says he's growing through his hair,
I know this isn't true.

Sheba is my friend's dog,
She lives next door to me,
When I go to see my friend,
She wags her tail for me.

Sheba is a collie,
Her coat is black and white,
It's silky soft and shiny,
Her teeth are big and white.

Sheba loves to see me,
I love to see her too,
She is very friendly,
She sits if I tell her to

Bryony Hall (7)
St Polycarp's RC Primary School, Farnham

The Minky, Manky, Monkey

I have got a monkey
Who swings in trees,
I checked his fur
And he's got fleas.

I took him to the vet's
So he could see,
He combed him thoroughly
And now he's flea free!

Claire Calvert (8)
St Polycarp's RC Primary School, Farnham

The Fox And The Hunt

The grass was shuffling where the fox was hiding
the hunter was coming his way.
Bang went the gun
the fox started to run
it ran through the field.
Bang went the gun.

It grazed the fox
the fox jumped through the bushes
everyone on the street was watching it.

The wind was blowing the fox's hair.
Bang went the gun
this time it hit its tummy
and it fell to the ground.
Goodbye Mr Fox
the hunt got you this time.

Myles Haddon (7)
St Polycarp's RC Primary School, Farnham

Snow

Snow before snowdrops,
Snowflakes falling down.
The sun comes up,
The sun goes down.
People play in the snow,
Cars go by them.
Children make snowmen,
Before running home.
When they go inside,
The snow melts away.
The children are sad.

Marcus Denny (9)
St Polycarp's RC Primary School, Farnham

My Cat Brandy

I have a cat called Brandy
I got her from the sanctuary
She was skinny
But we fattened her up
Soon she'll be as big as a truck
She likes a treat
And tinned meat
We were scared when she went out alone
But she came back in on her own
My mum gave her a groom
But Brandy spat
And sat on my lap
When I sleep, her tail
Wags against my feet
And then later on
She goes
On the sofa.

Holly Parsons (7)
St Polycarp's RC Primary School, Farnham

The Fox

Creeping silently, low to the ground,
looking for food, a rabbit will do.
Something is shining up ahead,
let's have a look, *snap!* In the trap
and now he's put his foot in it.

Joshua Salter (10)
St Polycarp's RC Primary School, Farnham

What Would You Like For Dinner Tonight Master Monster?

Squidgy snails,
with slimy trails.
Sludgy mud,
with soggy bugs.
Greasy goose,
with outdated mousse.
Mangy mice,
with stinky spice.
Squidgy brain squash,
with hands that aren't washed.

Bash it, mash it, stir it, whirr it,
get a bit of porridge and scrape it on a biscuit.
Hurl it, whirl it, mix it and unfurl it,
take a big fat spoonful and gobble it all up.

Patrick Edmondes (7)
St Polycarp's RC Primary School, Farnham

The Bun Man

The bun man had such fun,
He'd stick his thumb up to everyone,
To say, 'Hi,' as he passes you by,
He'd run and run to deliver you a bun,
So you could fill your tum.

The bun man had such fun,
To see your faces when you were full,
He was happy for you all,
Chocolate, cream, apple and jam
Whatever you wish he's your man.

Aimee Cunningham (8)
St Polycarp's RC Primary School, Farnham

Me And Silky The Bird

I was leaving from Scotland to a land that had never been discovered.
The sea was frozen.
I looked up to the misty sky,
I saw a bird that had silky, shiny skin.
The bird was my only company.
We sailed for a month and a day, just me and him.

One dark, misty night, a flash of lightning struck my mast.
A terrible storm rose from out of nowhere.
A giant tidal wave hit my boat.
I was terrified.
I could not see my companion in the black sky.
I thought he was lost forever. I was sad.

The sun came out. The storm had gone.
I looked into the clear blue sky and I saw my companion.
I was happy that he was alive.
Me and my companion sailed away to a faraway land.

Philip Barton (8)
St Polycarp's RC Primary School, Farnham

HARRY THE CAT

I love Harry the cat,
He sleeps on a furry mat,
For 20 hours or so
And loves to curl up low.

When he awakes
He stretches and shakes
And gets out of his basket for dinner
Look it's tuna, what a winner!

He loves to play with string
Then lets it go, *ping!*
He loves to play with wool,
He's ever so cool!

He runs through the cat flap
And after running about takes another nap,
In the warm sunshine
When the weather is fine.

I love Harry the cat,
He is so jolly and fat!
He always puts a smile on my face
When he plays chase.

Lauren Fernandes (7)
St Polycarp's RC Primary School, Farnham

My Dream Dog

My dream dog would do my homework,
He would do the washing up,
He would paint the house,
He would hang up the curtains
And let the guinea pigs out.
He would clean the windows,
He would enjoy my reading book
And polish every nook.
I would make him dust everywhere
And clean my room from top to toe.

If only this were true.
My own dog is quite the opposite.
She sleeps most of the time.
And the rest of the time she eats and plays.
Of course she does get up to go for walks!

My dream dog is somewhere else
If only he were here,
I suppose I could just start training the one I have
and love.

Esther Marshall (7)
St Polycarp's RC Primary School, Farnham

SCHOOL DINNERS

Oh mince! You are so yucky,
I've hated you since
You made me want to chucky.

Oh meatballs and rice,
You are not very nice,
The rice is dry and hard,
The meatballs are too squashy,
I'd rather run a thousand yards.

Oh hot dogs you are so tender,
Oh apple pie you are so juicy,
With a crunchy crust,
I could eat you both
Until I bust!

Shaun Sutehall (7)
St Polycarp's RC Primary School, Farnham

THE SEASIDE

I like going down by the sea,
That is where I like to be.
I like the sound of the crashing waves,
I could listen to it for days and days.
I like digging with my bucket and spade,
When it gets hot I sit in the shade.
In the sea I paddle all day,
I jump and swim and laugh and play.
In my bucket I put shells,
Until I hear the ice cream bells.
I choose the best one I can find,
Then we go home and leave the sea behind.

Sophie Smith (7)
St Polycarp's RC Primary School, Farnham

The Seasons

Winter is cold and is here three months of the year,
Him and his wife, Madam Snow,
Walk down the icy road.
Madam Snow is as white as blossom
And lays down a blanket of snow.

Miss Spring gives life to trees and plants,
She wakes the animals from their long winter rest.
Miss Spring asks the birds to sing and rejoice,
'Everyone it's spring, everyone it's spring!'

Master Summer is out today,
Rejoice, rejoice, for the fun and games.
Laughter's heard everywhere.
Everyone play,
Everyone rejoice this happy day.

Autumn is wet and damp.
Autumn kills the plants.
Who would have known it's only just been summer,
It seems to be a lifetime away.

Brendan Wright (11)
St Polycarp's RC Primary School, Farnham

In The Jungle

In the jungle
snakes hiss loud.
Lots of monkeys
make a crowd.

In the jungle
tigers roar.
Leopards crawl
across the floor.

In the jungle
parrots cry.
Toucans begin to fly.

In the jungle
giraffes eat.
Animals hate
the high heat.

Amy Gellatly (10)
Tillingbourne Junior School

Her Name Was Pearl

A fair young maid there was of old,
Her silver raiment shone,
Her mantle white was hemmed with gold,
She ran as swift as a swan.

A star was bound upon her brows,
A light was on her hair,
As sun upon the golden boughs,
In Mirridor the fair.

Her hair was long, her limbs were white,
Like a tender birch tree,
To behold her was a sight,
Of great rarity.

The villagers in harmony,
For so many years,
But then she left fair Mirridor,
Leaving them in tears.

'Farewell,' she cried
And as the people wept and waved,
The boat went sailing on the tide
And the people turned away and grieved.

Katie Hedgecock (10)
Tillingbourne Junior School

Guy Fawkes Night

This is the night when fireworks fly
Suddenly crackling Catherine wheels spin brightly.
Rockets racing across the sky, *bang,* sparkling,
Crowds of people munching sausages.

This is the night when fireworks fly
When the sparkling stars shine in moonlight at night.
Crowds of people munching peanuts at night,
When muddy wellies get mucky and icky.

This is the night when people shout,
Suddenly gorgeous smells come from the field.
Massive torches light up the field and fire,
Then racing Catherine wheels spin, shining.

Kathryn Giddins (10)
Tillingbourne Junior School

SHE USED TO SIT BY THE APPLE TREE

She used to sit by the apple tree,
Eating honeycomb from the honeybee.
Whose song was as merry as the nightingale
And her dance was light as the elfin mail.

She'd skip and run like the elfin folk,
She would dance and sing, but never spoke.
A rustle of leaves was the rustle of her dress
And her silken hair was never a mess.

She was the sparkle of the moonlight,
She was the glitter of stars at night.
The beams of light from the sun.
So bright was she that she shone.

She used to sit by the apple tree,
The light of happiness to the others was she.
Time went by and she disappeared,
That was what the folk often feared.
Her name was Dawn, who brought others glee,
She was the one who used to sit by the apple tree.

Carmel Heeley (11)
Tillingbourne Junior School

PARTED

We used to run together through the
waving grasses gold,
We used to climb each steepened side
of rocky mountains old,
We used to jump the river where the
silver fishes dive,
We used to eat the honey from the
honeybee's hive.
We used to pick the flowers from the
grassy meadows wide,
We used to watch the moon and sun
control the blue-green tide.
We used to hold each other tight
and pray to God above,
That we would stay forever together
in this glorious circle of love.

Emma-Jane Walker (11)
Tillingbourne Junior School

How The Morning Opens

The morning wakes from her dreamless sleep,
Her rays writhe into the sky,
Gleaming beautifully as she goes.
She glows like the embers on the fire,
She is the red, hot, amber stone, glistening in the sky,
The clouds appear, as night fades away.

The dewdrop trickles down the veins of the cherry tree leaf,
It falls and lands on the crippled bark of the tree,
It runs along the creased, rough surface of the bark.
It drops onto the fresh green grass,
As it joins its friendly, wet, dew mates,
It catches the sun's glowing light as it rises into the newborn sky.

When the waking of the morning comes,
The birds sing their morning song
And behind each musical note there is a story.
Nature is the audience, the listener,
To each bird's colourful song,
Each bird is unique, so is its music.

The morning rises and the city awakes,
A couple of clatters are heard at first,
Abruptly, hustle and bustle is formed.
People flurry, from their streets
And arrive at each shop, in a hurry.
This morning has arrived, as every other day has.

Claire Anderson (10)
Tillingbourne Junior School

If I Were Not Me What Would I Be?

If I were not me
What would I be?
I would be a dolphin,
I would bathe in pleasure.
I could glide as soft as a bird,
Not be caught,
But live in style.
To see all the wonderful scenery
And to have the sun shining
On my shiny back.
I would jump through the oceans' hoops,
I would be as happy as can be.

Joanna Flashman (10)
Worplesdon Primary School

Somewhere In Our School Today . . .

A gang of bullies are teasing a lonely child.
A flock of chattering children are excitedly running to lunch.
A gaggle of jumping reception children are racing madly around at play time.
A pack of smart teachers are walking down the corridor carefully.
A group of hardworking dinner ladies are quickly getting ready for lunch.
A class of puffed out kids are sadly doing PE on a cold day.

Emily Piercey (10)
Worplesdon Primary School

SOMEWHERE IN OUR SCHOOL TODAY

24 intelligent mathematicians are working out fractions,
multiplications and divisions methodically.
A class of intelligent scientists are trying to work out
it there's air in a sponge.
12 imaginative artists are looking out of the window
as they draw a winter tree.
A pair of brilliant historians are travelling back to
Tudor times to see what they did for a living.
2 brainy detectives are trying to find out what happened
yesterday by looking for clues.
A couple of clever reception class builders are building
a tower out of blocks.
A stampede of fit athletes are running around the field
training for a cross-country race.

Georgina Atkinson (10)
Worplesdon Primary School

THUNDER

Thunder is a giant
A roaring, howling mass of cold,
It hammers for almost ages
Raining showers of gold.

It stomps around the sky
And destroys everything in its path,
It slices down trees
Striking with his staff.

The sun's battling to no avail
In comes the rain, down comes the hail.
The thunder slips away into the background
And now the rain is the only sound.

Georgina Pollard (10)
Worplesdon Primary School

A Brilliant Recipe

Firstly, take a bowl and then take a handful of girls
playing with hair, into another bowl of chair swingers.
Next, whisk them around until they are dizzy.
Then add a pinch of cheeky children.
After that, sprinkle a tablespoon of doodling bad boys
and stir them until they dissolve.
Meanwhile, mix a bowl of tatty working children
and answering back children.
Shortly after, check how the girls are doing and then
add a hint of ink blotted homework.
After you have done that, add a small wedge of
note-sending children into an oven and leave them
there for twenty minutes.
There you have it, your own brilliant recipe.

Melissa Bundy (9)
Worplesdon Primary School

Somewhere In Our School Today . . .

A couple of athletic children are happily sprinting
around the field, training for their next football match.

A class of clever children are trying to write a brilliant
poem about the snow.

A group of exquisite poets are working on the last line
to finish their poems.

A dozen fit, athletic people are running as fast as they can
to win the marathon.

Adam Way (10)
Worplesdon Primary School

Somewhere In Our School Today . . .

A cluster of intelligent historians are learning how the
Tudors built their huge houses.
A great stampede of healthy athletes are coming back
after their races.
A class of imaginative authors are writing the next paragraph
of their story.
24 mathematicians are working hard at their tables.
A pair of creative artists are working really hard on their
sparkly winter trees.
A group of clever poets are performing their magical poems.

Kathryn Willis (10)
Worplesdon Primary School

Somewhere In Our School Today . . .

A dozen clever historians are finding out how the Tudors
lived when Henry VIII ruled.
A team of fit athletes are bravely trying to climb a long
rope in the hall.
A pair of brainy detectives are curiously searching through
a web page, trying to find out about the human body.
A group of intelligent masterminds are almost in the final
to win the game at wet play.
A bundle of enthusiastic players are trying to block the
others from winning a game of mini-rugby.

Victor Colombo (9)
Worplesdon Primary School

SOMEWHERE IN OUR SCHOOL TODAY . . .

A group of intelligent authors are thinking of a snappy slogan
to advertise a new food.

A group of enthusiastic poets are writing ideas in their books
as they try to compose a poem.

A couple of mathematicians are intelligently working out
a sum by counting on a number square.

A crowd of curious detectives are trying to work out
a word problem in maths.

A budding athlete is trying really hard to jump a fence in
PE.

A curious archaeologist has found a dinosaur bone.

Luke Riley (10)
Worplesdon Primary School

SOMEWHERE IN OUR SCHOOL TODAY . . .

A cluster of creative artists are using charcoal and chalk
to draw silhouettes of winter trees.

A pair of masterminds are clicking the mouse as they try
and find some interesting information about the human
body.

A team of swimmers are doing front crawl and trying to
achieve their swimming certificate.

A pair of actors are enthusiastically practising their
act for the school play.

A class of inquisitive mathematicians are finding new
ways to multiply big numbers.

Yasmine Cockram (9)
Worplesdon Primary School

SOMEWHERE IN OUR SCHOOL TODAY . . .

A crowd of clever mathematicians are sorting out hard word
problems methodically at their desks.
2 intelligent historians are going back in time to the Tudors
and Stuarts to see how they lived.
A team of healthy athletes are trying to win the long jump in
games.
A dozen imaginative scientists are working out what is a
solid, liquid or gas while sitting at their desks.
3 fantastic artists are looking at a photo and sketching
winter trees.
A couple of brilliant poets are writing an acrostic poem about
snow at the table.
24 imaginative authors are writing a story that is going to be
read out loud to their parents in a special assembly.

Rianne Dillon (9)
Worplesdon Primary School

A RECIPE TO MAKE YOUR PARENTS CROSS

Take a handful of slamming doors with a hint of messy rooms.
Stir a cupful of not doing homework with a touch of hitting
my brother.
Crumble a teaspoon of answering back with a drop of rudeness.
Bring to the boil whilst shouting at them.

Natalie Hamblin (9)
Worplesdon Primary School

TENSE MOMENTS

And here she is, her eyes fixed on the frisbee
Watching every move it makes,
Wait, has it? Will it? Is it? Yes!
The frisbee has been thrown,
Soaring through the air, what a blast
And of course the dog is racing behind it.
My word, she is in tremendous form,
But oh no, she is racing, yes racing,
Towards the polished area on the floor
And oh no, she has skidded,
But yes, yes, she's back up
And yes she has jumped,
Jumped and caught the frisbee
And landed on all four paws.
She has won the world record
Yes, what a performance
Absolutely brilliant
Another record won
Extraordinary work.

Bethany Cashmore (9)
Worplesdon Primary School

THE THUNDER TIGER

Thunder growls as it pounces across towns and cities unexpectedly.
Slowly, the thunder tiger stalks its unwary prey,
King of the sky as it prowls over the world,
Digging its yellow teeth into people's houses,
Thrashing violently with its muscular body.

Jacob Slyfield (9)
Worplesdon Primary School

Bonfire Night

Wizard fireworks give you a spark,
You will be watching them in the dark.
You will be very glad you came,
To see the fireworks flame.

They were the best,
Better than the rest,
I love to see the flying things,
They fly as high as wings.

Rockets blast up in the sky
And then the fireworks start to fly.
It is excellent to watch them flash,
Then they end in a great big crash.

Rhiannon Jennings (8)
Worplesdon Primary School

Wind

I taste the fruity rainbow as I glide through it.
I sit on a cloud,
and watch it blow away my thoughts.
Whispers soft blue secrets to me,
howling in the moonlit skies.
Let it parade through your caring heart.
Wild combinations of winds and curiosity,
locked away in a secret cloud-covered castle
of loneliness, sadness and tears.

Zoë Makin (9)
Worplesdon Primary School

FIREWORKS

Fireworks were whizzing,
Now they are fizzing.
They bash and they crash
And some of them smash.
They howl
And they growl,
They crack,
So stand well back.
They squeak and they creak.
Some fireworks are dizzy
And start to look whizzy.
Some clang and bang.
Tired toddlers are taken home
And then they start to moan.

Becky Nash (9)
Worplesdon Primary School

I WISH

I wish I wasn't so slow at running,
I wish I could fly to the moon,
I wish I wasn't very cunning,
I wish I could bend a spoon.

I wish I was very rich,
I wish it was Christmas every day,
I wish I could stitch,
I wish the other girls would let me play.

I wish I could touch the stars,
I wish I could make it snow,
I wish I could see Mars,
I wish I could make cakes out of dough.

Eloise Anders (8)
Worplesdon Primary School

COMMENTATOR

And she rummages through the basket,
Her hands touch something familiar.
She grabs the hairbrush,
Will she do it?
Will she brush her hair without being disturbed?
Will she?
Madly she starts to comb her hair,
Getting faster,
Even faster,
Until.
Why, what's this?
She drops the hairbrush.
It starts to roll downstairs.
Oh no!
Poo!
Her sister clenches the hairbrush in her hand.
What is she going to do?
She looks mad with rage.
She's preparing for a frog leap.
Wow!
Crash!
Is this the end?
Maybe next time.

Lauren Roberts (10)
Worplesdon Primary School

If I Were Not Me

If I were not me
What would I be?
I would be a seagull
Fly to Buckingham Palace
To see the Queen.
I would fly over the sea
And peck bread from tourists.
I would catch fish
I would glide over the ocean
And make admirers dizzy by circling
Around and around.

Michael Cook (10)
Worplesdon Primary School

Bonfire Night

Exploding and bursting in the night,
They really do make lots of light.

Catherine wheels spin round and round,
Like flying saucers on the ground.

Roman candles crack,
While we stand back.

Laura Cunningham (9)
Worplesdon Primary School

THE COMMENTATOR

And he's off . . .
Quickly and slyly he walks round the school.
Will he make it in time for class . . .?
Yes he has . . . that's astounding!
But wait, what's this . . .?
The teacher doesn't look too happy.
She raises a finger and is pointing to the homework box.
Oh no! His homework isn't there.
Quickly he's looking through his bag.
Phew, he's handing in his book.
The teacher's looking through it.
Wait, his homework's not in it.
Where is it?
His teacher seems pretty mad.
Oh no!
He's staying in after school.
This surely means disqualification,
Just as he was about to break the record.
Oh well
Back to the studio!

Holly Cooper (10)
Worplesdon Primary School

EARTHQUAKE

The Devil stamping, getting revenge.
Taste of death slow and painful.
Sound of Hell opening
Waiting for you to fall in
And stay there for all eternity.

John Sutcliffe (9)
Worplesdon Primary School

If I Moved House

If I moved house I would take . . .
My old school life,
The sight of laughter as the sun sets,
The taste of the fresh foxglove that my mum never
knew she had grown.

If I moved house I wouldn't take . . .
The sound of police cars rushing past my street,
The taste of burnt burgers and chips for tea,
The times of argument.

If I moved house I would take
the feel of the long grass on the common.
If I moved house I wouldn't take
the screech of the cats next door.
But if I moved house I would take
the washed smell of my neighbour's room.

Rhiannon Williams (9)
Worplesdon Primary School

Sea

Sea is like . . .
A tornado tossing boats and ships way up into the air,
Bowl upon bowl of over-salted chips,
Calling dolphins, jumping over waves,
Busy children searching for shells,
Sea comes in splashing at our toes,
Golden sands piled up by the waves,
Ice creams sat there waiting to be collected.

Jennifer Smith (9)
Worplesdon Primary School

Lightning

It shoots its claws down scratching the sky,
As if to try to pull itself down from its prison in the sky.
Waiting . . . waiting . . . waiting . . . it strikes out at its prey.
It thrashes about in the sky trying to escape from its cloudy den.
Then after a few minutes it roars with rage as if to try to
shatter the clouds.
An ear-shattering boom explodes in the sky, as it prowls around
waiting to strike again.
Its black shadow lurks in the sky watching everything.
Its mystery questions the mind.

Rory Whitby (9)
Worplesdon Primary School

What White Is!

White is a cloud, soft and fluffy.
White is snow, lying gently on the ground.
White is a wedding dress, with silky laces and
diamond necklaces.
White is paper, stories with blank pages.
White is a barn owl gliding across the moonlit sky.
White is coral, resting on the sand of the Caribbean Sea.
White is the daisy, producing colour on a sea of grass.
White is blossom, growing on the trees in my back garden.
White is the colour of the vanilla stains on my blue T-shirt.

Rachel East (10)
Worplesdon Primary School

SOMEWHERE IN OUR SCHOOL TODAY . . .

One single, hard-working caretaker silently sweeping up
after lunchtime.
A class of amazed scientists quietly making lots of different potions.
A gaggle of fashionable girls quietly whispering their secrets.
A gang of boisterous bullies secretly sneering behind people's backs.
A huddle of chatty teachers sitting noisily in the staffroom.
A queue of terrible boys waiting patiently for their lunch.

Eleanor Ellis (9)
Worplesdon Primary School

SOMEWHERE IN OUR SCHOOL TODAY . . .

A gang of boisterous bullies viciously picking on little kids.
A crew of moaning dinner ladies busily chattering away and not doing their work.
A river of quiet mathematicians cautiously looking up at the bellowing teacher.
A gaggle of giggling reception children eagerly waiting for their lunch.
A bunch of exhausted teachers scribbling quickly on the board.

Meghan Luxford (9)
Worplesdon Primary School

FIREWORKS

R aining down like snowflakes
O riginals are the best
C atherine wheels spinning
K ites of beauty filling the sky
E normous colours exploding high
T remendous displays of exploding sound.

Daniel Linington (8)
Worplesdon Primary School

If I Moved House

If I moved house I'd take . . .
The birds that woke me up early in the morning.
The smell of the salt in the sea.
The neighbours that came and said hello.

If I moved house I wouldn't take . . .
The alarm that went off during the night.
The water outside that nearly came in our house,
The neighbours complaining when we had our music up loud.

If I moved house I would take . . .
The different colours of the sunset,
The Christmas tree glowing in the dark,
The birthdays that we would celebrate.

If I moved house I wouldn't take . . .
The darkness trying to get me,
The wind howling in the night,
The heavy rain banging against the window.

If I moved house I would take,
The water fights in our garden.

Danielle Almond (10)
Worplesdon Primary School

Earthquakes

A massive pneumatic drill under the earth, pushing the ground aside.
A booming sound, ripping apart people's ears.
A punch of anger, trickling down your spine.
The trembling feel of an earthquake, he's like a huge giant jumping
up and down.
A huge monster releasing his ultimate power.

Jack McCarty (10)
Worplesdon Primary School

LIGHTNING

It shoots its claws down,
Scratching the Earth as if pulling itself down
From a prison in the sky.

Waiting . . . waiting . . . waiting
Strikes out at its prey.

It thrashes about in the sky
Trying to escape from its cloudy den
Then after a few minutes it roars with rage
As if to try to shatter the clouds.

An ear-shattering boom explodes in the sky
As it prowls around waiting to strike again.
Its black shadow lurks in the sky watching everything.

Its mystery questions the mind.

Thomas Adamson-Green (10)
Worplesdon Primary School

THE THUNDER TIGER

Thunder growls as it crosses towns and cities unexpectedly.
Slowly the thunder tiger stalks its weary prey.
King of the sky it prowls over the world,
Striking with its spiky yellow teeth, destroying the Earth.
Thrashing about it shakes the towns and cities with its muscular body.

Sebastien Toghill (10)
Worplesdon Primary School

If I Were Not Me, What Would I Be?

If I were not me,
What would I be . . . ?
A Billy goat.
I would eat the luscious green grass,
I would roam the lands
In my own time.
I would have scruffy, long shaggy hair.
I would stand on the edge of a cliff
And gaze out into the space of nowhere.

Chris Dempsey (10)
Worplesdon Primary School

Birthday

B rilliant pressies today.
I am so glad it's my birthday.
R ip of the paper
T oday is my birthday
H appy birthday to me
D ecorations everywhere
A ll the people surround me
Y es it's my birthday
S o sing out with joy, it's my birthday.

Nicole Fitzsimons (11)
Worplesdon Primary School

THE COMMENTATOR

And she's off
into the midst of a single room
one of the hardest challenges yet.
Oh, it doesn't look very promising
but
the basket is
right across the
other side of the room
she has to reach it or
she will get detention.
Can she?
Will she?
Is this the end
of an extraordinary
adventure?
Oh my word what skill
this young girl has
wait!
She has just tripped up
over a chair leg
yes a chair leg
she's struggling to get up
but she does it
with a badly hurt stomach
oh I hope she is OK.

Can she reach the
basket in time?
well I don't know
but I think she will
be OK.

Yes what a
performance she
has made it.
Well that's all
from me
back to the studio.

Emily Moon (10)
Worplesdon Primary School

If I Were Not Me

If I were not me,
What would I be?
I would be a giant tiger
Pouncing on my prey.
I would run as swift
As a bird soaring in the sky.
Lord of the forest,
Faster than a cheetah.
As I roar the trees would
Shake in horror.
I would have stripes
To the very tips of my tail.
My teeth would sparkle in the light.

Rosie Bowler (10)
Worplesdon Primary School

If I Were Not Me

If I were not me
What would I be?
I would be a horse.
I would be a horse that gave my rider pleasure.
Graze on Dartmoor,
Trot through the streets of Cornwall,
Glide through the woods.
I would be a happy horse
Galloping through the sand on the beach.

Sophie Maynard (11)
Worplesdon Primary School

If I Were Not Me

If I were not me
What would I be?
I would be a tiger
Killing mammals.
King of the forest.
So if you come hunting this way
Watch out!
There may be a tiger about.

Thomas Sands (11)
Worplesdon Primary School

The Thunder Tiger

The thunder tiger pounces,
As he digs his sharp white teeth into his prey.

He prowls through the darkness.
Digging his claws in the dirt, ready to roar.

He sneaks as he growls,
Thrashing about, looking around him.

The muscular thunder tiger waits for his prey,
Evil, yellow glowing, shooting out his claws
Ready to dig into his prey.

The thunder tiger's stripes move about.
As thunder strikes down,
He shakes his prey savagely.

Rebecca Goldsmith (9)
Worplesdon Primary School

Thunder Tiger

T hunder is like a roaring tiger ready to pounce.
H unting down out of the clouds above.
U ltimate enemies.
N o one can escape his sharpened claws.
D aringly stalking his victim.
E nergetically he leaps to his cubs.
R ed blood dripping from a murdered mammal.

Katie Daniel (9)
Worplesdon Primary School

The Commentator

And she starts,
She's writing the first line,
What a performance she is already on her second line,
Will she make it to the third line in 30 seconds?
Will she?
Has she?
She has!
What's that, is it a spelling mistake?
It is,
Oh no.
This is surely detention?
Oh well,
Back to the studio.

Francesca Barwood (9)
Worplesdon Primary School